Points East and West

LIBRARY AND ARCHIVES CANADA CATALOGUING IN PUBLICATION

Title: Points east and west / Janet Barclay.
Names: Barclay, Janet, 1947- author
Identifiers: Canadiana 20250190265 | ISBN 9781988657400 (softcover)
Subjects: LCSH: Barclay, Janet, 1947-—Travel. | LCSH: Voyages around the world. | LCSH: Voyages and travels. | LCGFT: Travel writing.
Classification: LCC G465 .B38 2025 | DDC 910.4/1092—dc23

Copyright © 2025 Janet Barclay

All rights reserved. Except for use in any review or critical article, the reproduction or use of this work, in whole or in part, in any form by any electronic, mechanical or other means—including xerography, photocopying and recording—or in any information or storage retrieval system, is forbidden without express permission of the publisher

Cover illustration: Map Resources
Cover design: Loose Cannon Designs

Published by
LOOSE CANNON PRESS
info@loosecannonpress.com

www.loosecannonpress.com

Points East and West

Janet Barclay

DEDICATION

Without the care and encouragement of the wonderful staff of the fourth floor at the Élisabeth Bruyère Hospital in Ottawa, the journey described in this book could never have taken place. I am forever in their debt.

TABLE OF CONTENTS

Dedication iv
Introduction   1
Chapter One: England   3
Chapter Two: Istanbul 17
Chapter Three: Singapore 34
Chapter Four: Bengaluru and Darjeeling 42
Chapter Five: Gangtok 60
Chapter Six: Return to Kolkata 71
Chapter Seven: Thailand 87
Chapter Eight: Return to Singapore 105
Chapter Nine: Sydney and Alice Springs 115
Chapter Ten: Uluru and Kata Tjuta 129
Chapter Eleven: New South Wales and Victoria . . . 142
Chapter Twelve: Sydney and Return Home 162

Introduction

Since our retirement several years ago, Bob and I have visited many fascinating places. We have explored a great deal of Canada and parts of the United States in our RV, and have seen and learned so much. And all the wonderful people we have met through our travels have made our journeying a joy. We have enjoyed taking our grandchildren on a couple of our trips, learning more about them, as well as allowing them to be introduced to the people and places we visit.

Outside North America, we have visited several of the major cities of Europe: Paris, Rome, Ravenna and London, and we have followed the Tour de France stage by stage. We have also seen many other smaller but equally exciting places. Our grandchildren have been part of some of these explorations. Watching their excitement in boarding a plane for an overseas trip was a joy. And the excitement of being somewhere else, where English or French were not the primary languages, was an education in itself.

Even so, with all these travels, we had not yet visited anywhere in Asia or Australia. Seeing these places became a goal. Our eldest son had lived in India for a couple of years and had told many stories about his time there; it was one of the countries we most wanted to visit. One of our son's good friends was now living in India, so visiting him and his family was a must. Another of our son's friends was living in Hong Kong, and had been hoping to see us at some point. We also had friends in Australia, so visiting them seemed to us a good idea. Now all we had to do was plan a trip, which would include stopping by with all these friends.

And so, the idea of a three-month jaunt around the world was born!

At first, we thought it crazy: the expense, the time away from home, and the enormous task of organizing it all. It was daunting at first look, but gradually it became more sensible, especially as we found we could use Aeroplan points to help us get on our way. The longest legs of the journey we planned would be flights of many hours, so we decided right at the outset that seats in the rear section of any plane would not be an option. Once we had accumulated enough Aeroplan points to afford the best seats in the house, it was time to book our flights. We wanted to escape the winter in Ottawa, so we planned to leave just before Christmas and head to London, UK, which would be the first of three travel hubs. We would stay there for a month, spending Christmas with our youngest daughter and her wife, and visiting a few places within easy reach. Then we would head off to Singapore, which would be our second hub, for travel to India and Thailand. After that, we would be back in Singapore before heading off to Sydney, Australia for the final hub of our journey. Finally, after visiting such places as Uluru and the

Great Barrier Reef, it would be time to head home to Ottawa just in time for spring. Oh, the best laid plans…

Tickets were bought and hotels booked—including a night in an underwater hotel on the Great Barrier Reef—all our friends were notified, and a couple of specific tourist attractions were secured, just to make sure. It was all very exciting. We made sure to get all our vaccinations for the various places we were visiting: prophylactic medications for malaria, just in case, and emergency medications we might need for a variety of potential health issues. Embassies and high commissions were contacted to ensure all our paperwork was in order. We created three-ring binders of documentation, a copy each just to be sure.

As all our long-haul flights were in business class, we were able to make use of the business lounges at our various hubs. As we sat in the departure lounge in Montreal, enjoying a glass of complimentary wine, we had difficulty believing we were actually on our way! It seemed like a long, suspended wait in the lounge until it was time to board. The plane left the ground, the wheels thumped in as we climbed, and our trip had officially commenced!

Chapter One: England

We left Ottawa on Dec 21st 2019. We had an early family Christmas at home, and then with all the decorations put away, and our bags all packed we were on our way. Excitement and trepidation were equally mixed. We would be travelling for three months right around the world, all our long-haul flights were booked in Business Class, thanks to Aeroplan, which made our life much more comfortable.

Our first flight left from Montreal, so a Greyhound bus from Ottawa was our mode of transport. We made it to Montreal in good time and relaxed in the lounge until our flight was called.

The flight was comfortable, and after supper we were both able to sleep for a couple of hours, which was a great relief. Our arrival at Heathrow was easy, we cleared customs and immigration quickly, and found the cab our daughter had booked for us. The driver was very friendly and talked all the way across London to our daughter's house. Fortunately, all we had to say was Um and Ah and Oh, yes? in the right places.

Our first day in London was spent just relaxing, catching up with family news, taking a short walk in the park so we could get used to the time change. A peaceful and calming interlude before the excitement of exploring some of the less usual sights of London.

We had seen the musical *Come From Away* in Ottawa, and really enjoyed it, so we bought tickets to the show in London and took our daughter and her wife to see it. I was interested in seeing how an English audience would enjoy the combination of Newfoundland humour and poignancy portrayed in the show. As always, it was very well received, and we all enjoyed it. For us a very worthwhile second viewing of this show

After the show, we enjoyed walking through the streets of the West End, enjoying the lights and Christmas ambience. As we walked through the cobbled streets, we took advantage of the vendors selling mulled wine and roasted chestnuts. Talk about a storybook experience!

We finished our rambling through the west end with a visit to Covent Garden. Not the open-air market of Eliza Doolittle, but rather a covered and heated market of the 20th century. The Christmas atmosphere was in full swing and a delight to experience. This lovely day finished with a delicious meal in an Italian restaurant, before we found our way back home.

CHRISTMAS EVE AT ST MARY'S

Now it was Christmas Eve, and our plan was to attend the children's Christmas service at our daughter's church. St Mary the Virgin dates from the 15th century, with many upgrades and changes. As we walked past all the present-day houses, we could only imagine what it must have looked like so many years ago. The verger gave us a guided tour of the crypt, no longer in use, and the church tower, both of which date back to the original founding.

The church was beautifully decorated for the season, but to our surprise there was no creche. Father Steve opened the service with a short welcome and introduction, during which he noted that the creche was not yet set up, but would be created throughout the service.

As the service proceeded children from the congregation brought the creche figurines in one by one, to be set in their appropriate spots, starting with a young boy and girl carrying the figures of Mary and Joseph. This was followed by a reading from one of the teenagers in the congregation, which set the pattern for the rest of service. It was quite delightful and was very inclusive of the children and youth of the church. Father Steve's sermon was wonderful and not like any sermon I have ever heard before. He started off by reading *How the Grinch Stole Christmas*! Not at all expected. He then related the end of the tale to the meaning of the celebration: Christmas isn't just presents, wrappings and food. Again, it was a very clever way to include the children while introducing the meaning of Christmas.

At the close of the sermon the children were called forward to make a living creche, so a small Mary and a tiny Joseph came up and sat down, followed by shepherds and three quite young little kings. All quite delightful. At the very end of the service, the children were invited up to receive a Christingle, a tradition we had not heard of before. The elements of the Christingle all have special meanings and relate the Christian story:

- The orange represents the world
- The red ribbon (or tape) symbolizes the love and blood of Christ
- The sweets and dried fruit represent all of God's creations
- The lit candle represents Jesus's light in the world, bringing hope to people living in darkness

The money raised from the sale of Christingles goes to help children in difficult situations, as did the collection from this service; a cause close to my heart.

After this delightful and unique service, we went home to our Christmas Eve supper. It was time to be with friends and family and enjoy those peaceful moments before Christmas day itself.

Christmas day was spent quietly. A lovely breakfast, which included crumpets shaped like Christmas trees, and then a long walk in the park, enjoying watching the kids playing with their new Christmas gifts: scooters, remote control cars, brand-new bikes. It was wonderful to see the joy in their faces as they learned how to use their new acquisitions.

Our day ended as it had begun, quietly. We called family in Canada and wished them all a good Christmas. We enjoyed opening and admiring presents, and in the evening, savoured really good food. We ended the day with champagne, and quietly went to bed, happy and relaxed after a lovely Christmas Day. After Christmas, when we had fully recovered from our jet lag, we were looking forward to exploring parts of **London** we hadn't seen. Our lovely ladies were off to Spain for a hiking holiday, so we were on our own for a few days.

Mithraic Temple

London is a city of many layers. Over the centuries, buildings have been lived in, built on, covered over, and rediscovered. Our first exploration was a visit to a Roman temple to Mithras, which was under the Bloomberg Building in the heart of the city.

The history of this temple in remarkable. It was deserted around the 3rd century CE, and over the course of time became lost and buried. During World War II parts were exposed as a result of the bombing during the Blitz, and then lost again to be rediscovered in 1954. The temple was eventually moved away from its original location, and in the excavations in 2010-14 for the Bloomberg project it was moved again and placed close to its original location, approximately seven metres below street level and underneath the Bloomberg building itself. Quite the story of discovery and restoration.

In the building foyer, we were shown a wall of artifacts discovered in the ruins, the variety of which was quite fascinating, then we went down a level where there was more information about the temple. Finally, down another level, we came to the temple itself. At the end of this quite large space, with columns on both sides, was a reproduction of the altar of Mithras and the Bull. The original altar is displayed in the British Museum, along with many of the artifacts found during excavations. As we entered the temple, we were given a short sound-and-light show which represented the religious service that might have occurred. The documentation for this show was derived from another temple discovered elsewhere.

The mithraeum's subdued lighting and some of the artifacts recovered

Not long after we left the mithraeum, we came upon a beautiful Christopher Wren church, St Stephen Walbrook. We stepped in and admired the interior domed space. It was really lovely and, in some ways, reminded me of the displaced Wren church we had visited in Fulton, Missouri in its simplicity and beautiful balance.

THE GUILDHALL AND ROMAN AMPHITHEATRE

After a quick lunch we found our way to the Guildhall and the Roman amphitheatre below it. On the plaza in the forecourt of the Guildhall was a large outline in black paving stones that showed the size of the original amphitheatre below. It was huge. We entered the Guildhall Art Gallery, and then descended to the level of the excavations

The actual excavations open to the public are small, but even so they are fascinating. It is possible to see some of the wall of the amphitheatre, areas where doors likely gave access to the gladiators, and perhaps the animals they had to fight. The wooden sewer pipes below the arena were also visible through glass floors. It is always interesting to see how the Romans managed these necessary things.

A section of the amphitheatre wall with its subdued lighting

Then it was up to the art gallery. There were some lovely paintings on display, and we enjoyed studying at them. While we were there, an art tour had just started. We chose not to follow the tour, but we enjoyed listening to the very long, art-historical analysis of one particular painting, as we sat and admired other ones. Shades of university art history lectures, better forgotten. We were relieved we hadn't signed on!

This was the end of a very interesting day of exploring just a small section of the underground life of London. A couple of days of relaxation later (and having caught up with family and done those necessary chores of any long vacation) we went into central London again, with the intention of visiting The Shard. This is a sharp, pointy building and the tallest in London. We were not successful! The line-up for tickets was extremely long and snaked around and around. It seemed that everyone thought the Christmas break would be the best time to see London from on high!

Our failure to ascend the Shard turned into a wonderful experience. As we wandered away, we came across the Borough Market, a very busy place with a plethora of foods on sale. The market itself is located under the arches of the main railway line, and the trains passing overhead can be heard and felt while you wander through the stalls. An interesting feature of this place.

SOUTHWARK CATHEDRAL

Much to our delight, once through the market we came upon Southwark Cathedral. This is thought to have been a place of worship since the 7th century, although its first direct mention is in the Domesday Book of 1086. It was then the church of St Mary, which was later changed to St Mary Overie, which means 'across the river.' So, it has a very long history of worship up to the modern day. The building was designated the cathedral of the diocese of Southwark in 1907.

It is a wonderful place to visit and we spent a couple of hours just wandering around. We had an interesting talk with one of the guides, who spent a lot of time describing the cathedral before switching to politics, a hot and contentious topic in the post-Brexit era. Visitors are allowed to take pictures in the cathedral, but if they want to take more than one, they have to pay £2.00. The money goes to the support of the building, which we thought was a worthwhile cause, and I happily paid the requisite amount. Bob spent some time examining the organ, which was duly photographed.

The gothic vaulting of the nave was beautiful. The guide suggested we examine the aisle on the left side of the nave. It is gently curved to the right, supposedly to represent the way in which Christ's head fell to one side when he was on the cross. An interesting demonstration of the beliefs of the clergy so many years ago, if not later mythology.

Like so many churches of this period, the floor is paved with inscribed stones commemorating those buried there. Many of the stones had dates in the 17th and 18th centuries, which were still quite legible. There were several larger sarcophagi in the side aisles, including one wooden replica of a knight, thought to be the finest example of its kind in England. We were able to see the Nonsuch Chest of 1588, a wooden coffer for keeping church records, which is also famous as an early and excellent specimen.

As we left the cathedral, we walked along the north wall of the building to a point where an archaeological dig had exposed the foundations, right down to the traces of a Roman road. This road probably led to the wooden bridge that had spanned the river in Roman times, later built more sturdily, but still the only way across the river until the 18th century. Yet another indication of the depth of the city.

After we left the cathedral, we wandered back through the market and took advantage of one of its offerings: a chicken, onion and ham pie served us well for supper.

A fitting end to a very good day.

Eltham Palace

On New Year's Eve and it seemed appropriate to visit Eltham Palace. Most of these old buildings have long pedigrees, from their foundation to their present-day appearance. Eltham Palace is no exception. The first mention of this building is in the Domesday Book in 1086. At that time, it was a manor house belonging to William the Conqueror's half-brother, Odo, Bishop of Bayeux. It changed hands many times until 1295, when Anthony Bek, Bishop of Durham acquired it. He rebuilt the manor house and constructed the moat around it. In 1305 he presented the house to the future Edward I, and it remained in the hands of the royal family until the Civil War. Henry VIII spent much of his childhood there and later spent much money on the place. However, his interest waned as he became much more involved with Hampton Court. Extensive changes were made to the building during the royal occupancy, and it became one of the favourite homes of the regents for many years. Charles I was the last monarch to spend time there, and during the Civil War it received a great deal of damage and fell into disrepair.

The approach to Eltham Palace

The palace grounds were used for a couple of centuries as a farm with the buildings used by tenants. Later in the 19th century more buildings were added and steps were taken to save the original great hall. This wonderful building was being used as a barn right up to 1903! Repairs were made to the buildings over the course of this time, and in 1914 the roof of the Great Hall was reinforced with steel braces and reroofed by the Office of Works.

The Great Hall in four views

In 1933 the Courtauld family took the property on a 99-year lease and did extensive renovations inside the building and in the gardens. It has become a leading example of Art Deco design, with lots of 'modern' touches, including a central vacuum system dating from the 1930s. The woodwork is exquisite, especially the marquetry and inlays, and everything is beautifully renovated with clean and luxurious lines. The house has been compared to a hotel and in some ways, and it certainly reminded me of some of the hotels I have stayed at. The lines are clean but feel somewhat clinical. It did not feel warm and inviting. Probably when the Courtaulds were in residence it would have felt more welcoming. The dining and sitting rooms are large and it is easy to imagine the number of guests coming to stay at the house and enjoy whatever entertainment was on hand.

The exterior of the house has been described as 'Wrenaissance' in style, a nod to Christopher Wren. The exterior was partly inspired by Hampton Court Palace and was designed to complement the Great Hall. When approaching the building, I thought the columns looked more classical, not like the redbrick Tudor of Hampton Court. So, this was something of a surprise. It is a wonderful entrance to the house, and no doubt the effect the Courtaulds wanted.

I think the most interesting part was the Great Hall. This has been restored to the state it likely had in the 16th century. The roof is spectacular and the windows, with their motifs take one back many centuries. I could just picture the Court of Henry VIII meeting in that wonderful hall. This was a good way to spend the last day of 2019 and to get ready for the New Year.

Mail Rail

To start the New Year, we visited the General Post Office Museum and went for a ride on the Mail Rail. Much to our surprise we learned that in the early 20th century, the General Post Office (GPO) had an extensive network of narrow-gauge, automatic trains that took mail to the sorting locations under all the major railway stations. By the 1990s it was deemed to be uneconomical and was closed down, but the GPO laid plans to reopen the network as a tourist attraction. So, naturally we had to visit and take a ride. We squeezed into a tiny train and were conducted through the network in the vicinity of the Mount Pleasant Sorting Centre.

We rumbled through narrow tunnels, stopping every so often for sound-and-light shows on the history of this wonderful installation. It was a 'rattling good time' and totally un-expected! The tour lasts about half an hour, then as you leave you can visit the adjacent museum in which there are displays of original rolling stock and artifacts. You can even stand in a replica of a railway mail sorting car, sorting 'letters' into slots while the floor rocks and rolls realistically underfoot. We left feeling that this exhibition had shown us a completely different view of the underworld life of London.

The General Post Office Museum just across the road didn't have the same impact as the Mail Rail, but it was still very interesting to visit and enjoy. Here they have an extensive display starting from the founding of the Royal Mail in the Georgian period. There is an original stagecoach, a crazy 'penny-farthing' type mail carrier, a dispatch motor-cycle

(which really took Bob's fancy), and even a cute little Morris van from the '30s. A proud recent addition is a spread of information panels and videos on the 1963 Great Train Robbery, when over £1M in banknotes was heisted from a mail train north of London.

Visiting Hampshire

After our busy days exploring London, we took the train to visit Jeff, Bob's colleague from years ago, and his wife Denise. Our friends met us at the station and brought us to their attractive bungalow, with its lovely garden and conservatory. Jeff is into botany in a very big way, collecting rare seeds from all over the world. He is very serious about his hobby, while his wife, Denise, collects teddy bears and has several hundred of them in all shapes and sizes. The afternoon was spent just catching up with all the news over the last several years!

The following morning Jeff drove us all into Portsmouth where the Tudor ship the *Mary Rose* resides. We made our way to the Portsmouth Dockyard and found our way to the building housing *Mary Rose*. On our way to this remarkable ship, we saw several historic workshops, and made side visits to historic ships in dry dock. The most impressive is *HMS Victory*, the longest commissioned naval vessel in the world. It is still commissioned today, although unlikely to go to sea anytime soon.

The *Mary Rose* sank in the Solent in 1545 during a sea battle with the French. She had fired a broadside and was on a sharp tack when a sudden squall pitched her over. As the gun ports were still open, the sea rushed in and all was lost. Although the position of the ship was known—and salvage attempts had been made over the centuries—it was not until 1971 that divers located exactly where she lay. The ship was excavated underwater, cables and frames were secured, and with the aid of cranes and floatation bags, she rose to the surface in the early 1980s.

Half of the ship had been scoured away over the centuries by the tide, so what remains is most of the starboard side. The hull is now displayed upright on its keel in a huge building, surrounded by galleries of exhibits of the thousands of recovered artifacts. Because the ship heeled over, most of the movable items—from huge bronze and wrought iron cannon, right down to personal effects and the owners thereof—remained preserved in the starboard side lying on the seabed. There were so many artifacts and so much information that one single visit was nowhere near enough to truly take in what we had seen.

After lunch we drove to Gosport on the opposite side of the harbour, where we could see both of Britain's aircraft carriers, which were in port at the same time, an almost unique occurrence. It had been a very interesting day, seeing both the old and the new ships of Britain's navy.

WINCHESTER

We wanted to visit the Great Hall and see the famous Round Table, so we set off the following morning. Of course, the Round Table is not the fabled one of Arthur and his knights, but instead dates to around 1290 when it was commissioned by Edward I. It is a massive construction of oak made in many segments and weighing 1,200 kg. Much to my surprise, the table was hung up on the wall! It seems it was one way of displaying it and at the same time keeping it out of the way. The table itself was repainted during Henry VIII's time and the Tudor roses are much in evidence. It is a wonderful piece to see and admire. The Great Hall itself is splendid. It has been a law court throughout its long life and has seen many famous trials throughout this time, including an IRA trial in 1973. It was originally built by William the Conqueror after the Battle of Hastings, and the Great Hall was commissioned by Henry III who had dismantled the original. The recent stained-glass windows represent some of those who have been associated with the history of Hampshire and are quite beautiful.

In one corner there was a bronze statue of Queen Victoria, cast in celebration of her Golden Jubilee. It is rather a splendid monument. It is said the sculptor used his mother as the model for the figure, which struck me as a very homely touch. It was a very interesting visit, and although it was never King Arthur's court, one could imagine how his court might have fitted right into this beautiful space.

After enjoying the beauty of the Great Hall, we walked down the narrow High Street to Winchester Cathedral. The cathedral stands away from the High Street buildings in its own precinct. We hadn't been able to spot it until we came quite close because it has no spire, and thus doesn't loom above anything! It is a beautiful 13th century gothic edifice, built around the Norman church, parts of which can be seen in the transepts. A high-light of the visit was a chance to see the

great Winchester Bible, produced in the 12th century. It is in four massive volumes, each displayed in a glass case, and the pages are turned frequently. The writing is incredibly neat and precise, and it so consistent through-out that it is believed to be the work of just one scribe. The illuminated capitals and other figures are exquisite and the colours as vibrant as when fresh.

On our way out of the cathedral we came across a small chapel which had some wonderfully preserved frescoes from the 12th century. It is always a wonder how such things become preserved when so much rebuilding, alteration and demolition take place over the long life of the edifice. Perhaps more by luck than anything else, but it helps that frescoes were often whitewashed over, thus being preserved until rediscovered.

A lovely lunch in the Refectory concluded our visit, and then it was time to make our way back to the train station, and then to London.

TROY AT THE BRITISH MUSEUM

Before we left Canada, our children had given us a very different Christmas present: tickets to the Troy Exhibition at the British Museum. So once back in London, we took full advantage of this thoughtful gift and made our way to the museum.

Above: Terra cotta frieze
Left: A gladiator gets running repairs

The exhibition told the stories of the Iliad and the Odyssey through the medium of classical art, primarily ceramics but including frescoes, terra cotta and stone sculpture. The fineness and condition of many of the ceramics was wonderful, and we found it incredible that they have survived millennia in such good condition. The popularity and pervasiveness of these two great tales of antiquity was evident in the repetition of the themes through the Etruscan, Greek and Roman periods, and into the Middle Ages and the modern era. There was even a bas relief of the Trojan Horse in a Buddhist sculpture from northern India. The artifacts were beautifully displayed and thoroughly labelled, but we felt the low lighting gave a rather sombre effect. Few, if any, of the works were susceptible to fading and the lighting was largely LED anyway. It seemed to that the 'pools of light' display technique was more fashion than practicality. All in all, a fabulous exhibition and not to be missed.

While at the British Museum we visited the Anglo-Saxon gallery specifically to see the royal treasure from the ship-burial at Sutton Hoo in Suffolk. This is the richest archaeological find ever made in Britain, and the level of workmanship was astonishing. Gold, enamels, and inlays of precious stones decorated most of the king's war gear, and he had been buried with silverware, utensils, a purse of coins, and several emblems of office. Although his identity is uncertain, the burial dates to around 590.

After our visit, totally museumed-out, we made our way home since our feet were complaining and telling us to stop walking!

GREENWICH

With our feet recovered overnight, and together with our daughter and her wife, we were off to Greenwich in the morning. We took the bus to Lewisham where we connected with the Docklands Light Rail (DLR) which took us to Greenwich. This smaller railway was built during the construction of Canary Wharf and was designed to transport working people into that area. It is a cute railway, smaller than the regular railway and the Tube. The gauge is narrower, while there are tighter and more frequent curves and gradients. The trains are driverless, so it made sitting in the front rather interesting. You can watch the train go around bends, come up to stations, stop and start with no apparent input from a person! A bit disconcerting but perfectly safe.

At Greenwich we came upon the *Cutty Sark* in all its glory. This is one of the last of the great tea clippers and is preserved in dry-dock. Then it was off to the Pensioned Seaman's Institute to see the famous Painted Hall (previous page). The frescoes were painted in the early 18th century and the scope and detail is incredible. We spent quite some time there, learning all about the history and iconography of the works. There is so much to see in this one place, you could spend many happy hours just looking.

In the undercroft of the building, we came across a skittle court, set up as it would have been in the 18th century. We enjoyed bowling for the ten pins, making some considerable scores. Bob had a strike on his first ball![1]

Our last stop in this building was the Royal Naval Chapel, which is still in use today. It was designed and built by Christopher Wren and is a beautiful, simple, and very calming place to be.

Lunch was great that day. We stopped at a traditional pie and mash shop, with a side order of eels, which not all of us partook of! This was accompanied by great mugs of tea, so we were all well fortified for the afternoon's activities. We went back on the DLR, passing the O2 Arena, going under the Thames to the north bank, and eventually stopping at the Royal Dock. There we walked to the gondolas that span the Thames. The system was initiated by Boris Johnson when he was Mayor of London, but like  Johnson they really serve no useful purpose. They go from nowhere to nowhere, but what a ride! We sailed high above the Thames and could see quite a distance both up and down river. A lovely tourist activity, but not close to anything else! Then we took the boat from Greenwich up the Thames to the Embankment. A really lovely trip and a means of transport that has been used for many hundreds of years for moving people up and down the river.

While we were enjoying the gondolas and boat ride, our daughter had gone home to pick up our luggage for our trip to Istanbul. Our flight was early the next morning, so we planned to spend the night in a hotel at Heathrow. We met the girls with our suitcase, and stopped for a glass of wine near Covent Garden. We joined Bob's niece Cathy for a lovely dinner at an Italian restaurant, then it was goodbyes to all and off to Heathrow on the Piccadilly Line tube.

---

[1] On our return to Ottawa a couple of months later, Bob made a tenpin skittle court in our basement. It makes a fun activity in the winter!

Chapter Two: Istanbul

During one week of our stay in London, we took a side trip to Istanbul. This was a magical trip. Both Bob and I had seen pictures of all the great classical monuments of Constantinople, and now we were going there. We also had the joy of meeting our son David who was also doing some travelling, so we were able to share this experience with him.

On arrival at the Levni Hotel, right in the old city, we were regaled with at least half an hour of tourist information. The staff at the hotel were certainly eager to share all their knowledge with us.

We spent our first morning walking slowly through the streets, crossed over a tramway, and there before us was Hagia Sophia in all its glory. It was incredible to be actually seeing this wonderful building. The towers and domes and colours were marvelous.

As we continued walking though Sultanahmed Square numerous touts tried to sell us any number of tours, which we refused, and they backed off. As we continued our walk, enjoying this magnificent area, we passed through the gardens and saw vendors selling corn and other treats, which we planned to sample later. We passed the Mausoleum of Suleiman and wended our way through a network of narrow roads heading toward the Sea of Marmora.

Gradually we made our way around the Blue Mosque, which we intended to visit later in the week. I was quite taken by some beautiful carpets in a store window, and although the owner offered to sell me one and send it over to Canada on our return, he accepted our very firm refusal. However, those carpets were quite beautiful, and would have looked lovely in our living room.

TOPKAPI PALACE

We slowly made our way back towards Sultanahmed Square, with the plan to visit the Topkapi Palace. We came across a couple of obelisks, imported from Egypt by Emperor Constantine, in a long plaza that took us back to the gardens in front of Hagia Sophia, and so to the Topkapi Palace.

The front entrance of the palace is surprisingly understated

The Palace is a huge and wonderful complex. We went first into the kitchen areas, although we accidentally entered an area where the off-duty police were stationed! We didn't stay long as they ushered us out quite quickly. The kitchens are enormous, having to cater to the entire palace, with large fire areas, huge chimneys and oversized pots and pans for cooking. The serving dishes on display in glass cases were huge and beautifully decorated, made of metal and Chinese porcelain. This gave an idea of the enormous wealth of the Sultanate. Just trying to imagine producing meals for hundreds of people was mind boggling, and the catering was done on a regular basis for masses of guests, emissaries, and visitors. And even more so when important personages on diplomatic or political missions would arrive.

We continued our tour around the palace, visiting receptions rooms, audience halls, the throne room, and the Sultan's private mosque. Every building was decorated inside and out with glazed ceramic tiles, gold leaf and plasterwork. The effect was opulent and overwhelming. We could imagine the reactions of the visitors from far countries.

Some of the beautiful tile work that covered almost every surface

The throne of the sultan covered in embossed sheets of pure gold

HAGIA SOPHIA
Visiting Hagia Sophia was the goal of the following day. We had all studied this iconic building at some point in university classes, so actually being there was somewhat dream-like. We walked through the plaza and made our way to the public entrance at the side. Because our visit was in January, the line-ups for tickets to this, and all these great monuments, were relatively short. This is a relative term, as I can't imagine what it would be like with the crowds in the summer months.

What can I say about this wonderful building? It is overwhelming! It's hard to understand how such a colossal space could have been roofed over more than 1,400 years ago. Everywhere you look there is the soaring space of arches and domes, one on top of the other. We just wandered around admiring its beauty and enjoying the challenge of trying to take it all in.

The upper balcony gave a fine view of the nave. We walked up a zig-zag stone ramp (not suitable for wheelchairs, the notice said) which went round and round until we were at the top. We could look down onto the nave, which gave a quite wonderful perspective, as well as get another view of the domes and arches above us. At this level there were the remains of some Byzantine mosaics that Bob recognized from his art history studies.

One of many Byzantine mosaics in various states of preservation

Some areas of Hagia Sophia were inaccessible due to renovation work so. while our view was blocked, we appreciated that this will work is intended to preserve the building for future visitors. (The scaffolding towers can be seen on the previous page.)

After spending some time just absorbing the beauty and grandeur of the building, we went back outside and came across some excavated remains in an open trench, probably from the Roman period. We were not sure what they were originally as there was no signage, but they were now just one aspect of the history of this fabulous place. A little way away there was a large area with more Roman bits and pieces lying around. There was no information board here either to indicate what was planned for these pieces, which was a shame as we would have been interested in knowing.

As we left the precinct of Hagia Sophia we came across a rather splendid fountain, covered in gold. This was built in the 16th century after the building had become a mosque, for the ablutions of the faithful before they went in to pray. After this wonderful experience we walked through the plaza area just thinking about what we had seen.

THE BLUE MOSQUE

The Blue Mosque faces Hagia Sofia. Its structure is very similar to that of Hagia Sophia—in fact, the former laid the groundwork for general mosque architecture—and there are lots of marble columns, domes, and stained glass.

The building was open for visitors, so in we went. As the mosque is an active place of worship, we had to follow all the protocols. I had to cover my

head before entering the precinct, but fortunately my puffy jacket has a hood or I would have needed to borrow a headscarf provided by the authorities. Then, as we lined up to go in, we were stopped by a sign that told us, 'No shoes across this carpet.' So, everyone's shoes came off and we were given plastic bags to carry them in. One person tried to keep her shoes on by covering them with the plastic bags, but it was not allowed, so off they had to come. This necessary procedure must be a nightmare in the high tourist season.

The four main supporting columns of the nave are absolutely enormous. The picture on the left gives an idea of the scale

(Below) Mosaics of a side chapel where views upwards were less restricted

Half of the interior space was cordoned off for restoration work, but the protective coverings of the scaffolding structures had been painted to resemble architecture. Even so, the temporary structure made it impossible to see the dome in its entirety, and none of our photographs could do it justice.

BOSPORUS CRUISE
Our son David was travelling in the Near East, and took time to visit us for a few days. We had booked a boat ride up the Bosporus for the afternoon, and there was an interesting bus ride from the hotel to say the least! We were taken through narrow roads that should never have allowed buses, into places which seemed too narrow and tight, stopping at times for no apparent reason, until we finally arrived at the dock on the Golden Horn. We crossed a busy road, taking life and limb in our hands, and after walking down a small and

dirty alleyway, we found the boat. We were welcomed on board and directed toward a very well-appointed dining area for a buffet lunch. After lunch we went up on deck and enjoyed the warmth of the January sun, so much so my nose was distinctly pink that evening. Not bad for winter.

The boat headed out of the Golden Horn and up the Bosporus toward the Black Sea. The outward trip, against the flow, was fairly slow so the passengers were able to see various sites on the way, and there were many. We passed many palaces, mosques and other important buildings as we travelled along. At one point we were told that there were 3,600 mosques in Istanbul! Religion is a serious business here. With a population of 15 million people, it makes sense to have so many religious houses.

Quite a contrast between the traditional and the modern

Istanbul is one city on two continents: Europe and Asia are separated by the Bosporus. There are many bridges across this waterway for cars, buses, trams and trains. As we observed the city from the water, we could see just how closely the houses were packed together, and all higgledy-piggeldy up and down the hills that make up this crazy and wonderful city.

As we cruised slowly up the ancient waterway, we came upon many tour boats, Coast Guard ships, and lots of freighters going about their business. The Bosporus is the conduit between the Black Sea and the Mediterranean so the marine traffic is voluminous. We passed under many bridges and were amused to see how many people were fishing from them. Not sure what they caught, if anything, and from such a tremendous height.

Further up the waterway, we passed a large fort overlooking a narrower section. No doubt in years gone by this was important in protecting the city. Finally, we made it to the turning point of our trip, with the Black Sea in the distance ahead of us. We moored at a small fishing village on the Asian side of the Bosporus, where we could leave the boat for about 30 minutes. This gave us time for a walk and for our son to buy a fish sandwich from the local fishermen, as recommend by the boat crew. He said it was okay but needed more seasoning.

Once we were back on board, it was a much quicker ride back to our starting place. It was getting dark by this time and we watched the lights coming on both sides of the river. Once we had docked, we found our bus and headed back to the hotel. This trip had shown us a very different side of Istanbul. It is a busy port as well as a beautiful and ancient city.

THE GRAND BAZAAR AND SPICE MARKET

The previous day had been very busy and rewarding, so we decided to see another aspect of Istanbul. A visit to the Grand Bazaar and the Spice Market seemed to fit the bill. Our walk from the hotel was through narrow streets that had no level surfaces, dodging vehicles and hurrying people, and absorbing the sights and smells. After about half an hour we came to the gateway of the Grand Bazaar, passing through security before entering. The Grand Bazaar is a huge network of pedestrian ways that spreads over acres of land.

The crossing of two of the many intersecting covered streets

The whole complex is lined with stalls selling everything it is possible to imagine, and all under arcades and domes. In the corner of the main crossing (previous page) is the pulpit where the imam sings the prayers before trading begins. The merchants tended to be in concentrations, so in one street you'd find all textiles, next along handbags or clothing or trinkets, then whole rows of gold and gems. We were most attracted by the gold, which was there in abundance. There were also booths where gold was bought and sold, and for a price you could buy your very own stamped ingot or coin.

A gorgeous array of gold, either in worked pieces of jewelry or ingots and coins

The candy shops had profusions of the most exotic sweet-stuffs, with the signature Turkish delight everywhere. And all along our stroll through the bazaar we were petitioned by very persistent stall owners with wares for sale. We had never seen anything like this in all our western travels; it was a street market gone crazy.

The Spice Market was just a short walk away. This consisted of two intersecting covered walkways forming a cross, and again covered by arcades. As soon as we walked in, we were blown away by the smell of spices, all mingled together. Spices of all colours and textures were piled up in the stalls: heaps, pyramids, open sacks and bags, each with its own descriptive label. Just as the Grand Bazaar, it was like nothing we'd seen before; even the spice market in Campo dei Fiori in Rome—wonderful in its own way—did not come close to the extravagance of this one.

GALATA TOWER

We had seen the tower across the Golden Horn, built on a hill a tram ride away from our hotel. We crossed the Golden Horn from the Old Town and spotted the tower high above a cluster of buildings, and commanding a wide view. It was built in the 15th century as an observation post and lookout. The tower is approached by a series of steep cobbled roads and a staircase, with stores and houses all opening out onto these walkways. Once at the tower you can either take the stairs to the top, all nine floors, or take the elevator up to the seventh level and then climb the final two flights, which naturally were tight as they spiraled round the tower.

At the top is a very narrow external gallery, so one-way traffic is a must. The view over the whole area is spectacular and well worth a visit. The panorama of the Old City to the south is wonderful, as is the view to the north up the Bosporus. When we had seen our fill, Bob and David ran down the stairs while I took the elevator. They ended up waiting for me at the bottom! It just shows elevators are not always the quickest way down.

(Below) The view from the tower: Topkapi Palace and Hagia Sophia, with the Sea of Marmora beyond

The Cistern

David had seen a tourist information brochure on the Cistern and, as we had never heard of it, we were curious. And what a surprise it was. The Cistern was built for water storage in the 6th century by Emperor Justinian, and lost to the world for 10 centuries until rediscovered by a Dutch investigator of the 16th century who had interviewed people living above the structure. They showed him holes in the floors of their houses where they dipped buckets for water, and also did some fishing for their supper!

This is a huge underground structure supported by columns scavenged from earlier Roman and Greek ruins across much of the Empire. The columns sit on bases of marble, also taken from ruins, and support a vaulting of brick. The cistern is floored with brick cemented in place to make it waterproof. Water to fill it came via an aqueduct from the surrounding hills. When in use it could contain 100,000 tons of water, and once rediscovered, the cistern continued in use until the early 20th century when it was emptied and opened as a museum attraction. It is still very damp with groundwater, dripping continually. There are two famous columns that sit on sculptures of Medusa's head; one is upside-down, because this way it was the right height for the column it supported. The second medusa is sideways on, likely put this way for the same reason! I guess for an underground cistern, it was all about utility rather than beauty! However, there are a couple of romantic tales about these sculptures, the most likely one stating that the Medusa's heads were placed deliberately to provide protection for the building. Who knows, but as they have stood there since the 6th century, maybe they do?

The dripping water, the subdued lighting and spooky background music make the Cistern a very eerie place to visit. As we emerged and walked back along the road, we thought how weird it was to think of all the cars, buses, trucks, and people passing over an ancient water reservoir just six metres below the road. I wonder what Justinian's engineers would think if they could see their work today.

David planned to leave the next day for further adventures in Israel and Egypt, so we had a nice dinner in the hotel restaurant to celebrate our combined vacation.

Sultanahmet Square and Carpets

The following morning, we caught up with some of those required chores every vacation brings, and then went off to Sultanahmet Square again. We bought some delicious roasted corn from one of the many vendors, and then some bread treats to finish our rather interesting lunch. It was a great experience just sitting in the square and looking at Hagia Sophia as we were eating. It all still felt somewhat surreal.

After lunch we wandered along the park and started a conversation with a young man who is teaching English and likes to practice it whenever he can. He was a fund of knowledge about the history of this area and told us lots about it. The place where we had seen the obelisks was originally the hippodrome and stretched all the way to Hagia Sophia. The races used four-horse chariots, and they raced for seven laps around a long, looped track

There is a Serpentine Column in what was the central part of the course, made of bronze and depicting three intertwined serpents. It was used to signal the start of a race. A fire would be built at the base, and as soon as smoke was seen coming out of the serpents' mouths at the top, the race would start. The heads of the serpents were removed many years ago and are now on display in the British Museum.

The young man then led us to his family's store, revealing the real reason he had engaged us in conversation. Upstairs we were shown the carpets his family sells, and given apple tea and Turkish delight, both of which were excellent; lots of different kinds with a variety of flavours. The carpets were wonderful: finely hand-woven from silk and of all shapes and sizes with fabulous designs and colours. A wonder to behold. Some of them had taken over four years to make, as they were all done by hand. The workmanship was incredible; thousands of knots so close together to make these very famous designs. If you looked at some of them in one direction the pattern appeared to be made in lighter colours, turning it around the colours were darker. It is all to do with the way the light reflects off the nap. An incredible effect. There was one carpet I thought was particularly wonderful: it was a picture of horses galloping towards the viewer. Very realistic, and if I didn't know it was a small carpet, I would have thought it to be a painting. Another

one showed Noah and the Ark, with the animals done with tiny silk knots in lovely colours. I could have spent hours just looking at these works of art.
We were allowed to handle one of the smaller carpets, which felt so smooth to touch. A real silk carpet, a dream to have, but not at all practical in our house. We were given the hard sell but resisted. Maybe one day, but not now. However, the shop also sold a range of very fine spices, and as our son had requested some to take home, we ordered a few kinds. A box of Turkish delight went into our bag as well; the grandchildren would love it. We left the store loaded down with spices and Turkish delight and a host of delightful and unexpected memories.

We walked back along the hippodrome area and came to the Tomb of Sultan Ahmed Khan, who died in 1617. The tomb was built for him between 1617 and 1619. We went into the tomb, and out of respect we had to remove our shoes and I had to wear a head covering. It was a single, beautifully decorated room with the caskets belonging to the sultan and his family members, all appropriately labelled with their names. The Sultan's casket was of course the grandest one, while the others were fairly plain, and ranged from small ones for the many children, to average size for the adult members of the family. This mausoleum had a very different feel from Christian ones I have visited. I am glad to have seen it but seeing the caskets laid out that way, it seemed somehow that we were intruding, even though it was open to all who wish to enter. It seemed that such a private area was too easily accessible. I needed time to think about my reaction to it, and I am still not sure how I feel.

The Tomb of Sultan Ahmed Khan

CHORA MUSEUM

On our last day in Istanbul, we visited the Church of the Holy Saviour, which is now the Chora Museum. This museum/church is situated just inside the old city walls that cross the peninsula from the Sea of Marmora to the Golden Horn. We took a taxi for this visit and had the joy of a mini sightseeing tour along the shore of the Sea of Marmora. There were many freighters lying at anchor, indicating what a busy port Istanbul is. We were dropped off some distance away and walked through narrow streets to the church.

The church was consecrated in the 4th century, rebuilt in 11th century, and again in the 14th. There are traces of frescoes from the earlier period, and the mosaic decorations were added during the 14th century rebuild. After the Ottoman Empire conquered Byzantium in 1453 the church was converted to the Kariye Mosque. It remained a mosque until it was opened as a museum in 1945. When the church was converted to a mosque around the year 1500 the decorations were plastered over, which resulted in passive preservation. It was well-known for its Byzantine iconography, but a short time after our visit we heard that it—like Hagia Sofia—had been returned to a house of Muslim worship.

There are mosaics on just about every wall of this building and in the domes, arches, and vaults. The majority of the mosaics are complete and look as if they were created just a little while ago, while others show the depredations of time and need some imagination to visualize them as they were. One particularly interesting panel depicted an Ottoman princess who was 'given' to a Mongol chief as a peace offering, along with a whole load of goods and gifts. She found the Mongols to be close to animals in their eating, dress, and general deportment, so she set about teaching them manners. After many years the chief died, and she chose to return home to Constantinople where she founded the church.

After this interesting visit we walked along the outside of old city walls, happening to come on the very gate where the Ottoman conquerors entered Byzantium in 1453. This was quite unplanned, but added to the interest of this visit. We located a taxi near the gate. Our driver took a different route back to Sultanahmed Square, this time along the Golden Horn, which gave us another fleeting opportunity to see another side of this remarkable city.

The gate where the Muslim conquerors entered in 1453

THE ARCHAEOLOGICAL MUSEUM

Our last exploration of Istanbul was the Archaeological Museum. We had been told not to miss this museum, and after seeing it, we had to agree. The main collection is a series of sarcophagi excavated in the 1880s from a site in Syria. They date from the 5th and 6th centuries BCE and are huge and incredibly decorated. Most are sculptured on all four sides with lifelike figures such as battle scenes, horse races and cere-monies. It was astonishing that so much work would go into an art- work that would soon be hidden from sight.

An elaborate sarcophagus and one of the many tiled decorations in the Kiosk

The rest of the collection comprised sculptures, temple fragments, more sarcophagi and steles, from the Greek, Roman and Hellenic periods. All too much to take in on a single visit. This is a site that demands several visits.

After visiting the main museum, we walked across to the Tiled Kiosk. This little building is tiled through-out with a variety of intricate designs in many shapes and colours and is now used as a display space for ceramics. We saw some beautiful examples of ceramic crafts spanning about five centuries. It was here some of the sarcophagi were stored when they were first brought to Istanbul, before the museum was built. I think it was a perfect place for them to rest peacefully before their final home was ready.

This was the end of our explorations in Istanbul. It is a wonderful city and deserves much more time than the week we were able to take. Both of us would love to go back and spend several more weeks exploring further and revisiting many of the buildings we were able to see. Our visit just touched the surface of this remarkable place.

It was time to leave and make our way back to the airport for our flight to London and the last part of our stay there. We were sad to leave this interesting city, and maybe, just maybe, we will be able to visit it again in the future.

Chapter Three: Singapore

After our adventures in Istanbul, we returned to London for a week before flying to Singapore and the start of our adventures in the east. This was be my first time in this part of the world and I was eagerly looking forward to it, while Bob was keen to show me the sights from his brief visit to Singapore 10 years ago. We would only be in Singapore for a short time, but would return later in our travels.

We took a flight from London to Zurich, and changed planes for the 13-hour overnight flight to Singapore. Here the advantage of business class was profound; we were in adjoining pods, which had seats that could be flattened for sleeping. We were worried about how well we might sleep, but we needn't have worried. After supper we bedded down, and the next thing we knew it was breakfast time! We had slept well and found that we would be landing in Singapore in only two hours.

We arrived at 5:50 pm local time and, like almost every airport in the world, walked forever from our gate. No doubt it is very good for stretching stiff legs! Immigration, picking up luggage and customs clearance were very efficient, and then it was out into the warm tropical air of Singapore to find a taxi to the hotel. The reception staff upgraded us to a nicer room than the one we had booked; we weren't really sure why. The room was high in the building and overlooked the Singapore River, so one of the first things we did was take a walk along the riverbank and enjoy the warmth of the tropics. So different from the weather we had left behind in England and Canada.

Our first full day in Singapore was spent relaxing and pinching ourselves to remind us we were actually here. It really felt like a dream. We checked out all the restaurants along the riverside, and had a plate of humus and nacho chips for our lunch at one of them, our first meal in Singapore! We planned on trying another one for dinner that night. As we walked along the river, we heard a loud splash. We didn't see what had caused it, but the water was swirling. As we wondered what it could be, a couple of metres along we saw a sign warning people to look out for otters crossing the path. It made us wonder if the splash was an otter diving into the water. If so, we hoped we'd see these interesting creatures at some time during our visit.

Now to practicalities. Bob had to change money as, amazingly, the hotel didn't offer that service and the change machine in the foyer refused our pound notes. The nearest money exchange was in Mustafa Centre, a cab ride away and the only place open on a Saturday. This is a huge Indian market and is always very loud and active, and from Bob's brief visit it sounded like a wonderful place to return to. The rest of the day was quiet, catching up with my blog, taking short walks up and down the river, and generally relaxing.

That first evening we sat on the outside terrace of the hotel in the warmth with a glass of complementary wine each. A lovely aperitif before heading out to a lovely Italian restaurant we had seen, just was just a few minutes away from the hotel. The food was excellent and made a great finish to our first day in Singapore.

The next day, our first full day, was devoted to touristing. Bob bought tickets for the Hop-on Hop-off bus and off we went. To get to the bus stop opposite the hotel, we climbed a rather high pedestrian bridge that crossed the road. On the crossover part of the bridge there was an interesting notice, which said 'no riding on bikes, scooters or skateboards!' Just one of the many rules imposed on the citizens here.

The Botanical Gardens

The bus wove around the city, until it arrived at the Botanical Gardens, a place Bob told me was a 'must see.' As we learned when we arrived, the 162-year-old Singapore Botanic Gardens is a UNESCO World Heritage Site, and the only tropical garden to receive this honour.

Our first destination was the Orchid Garden, and walking towards it we passed a charming man-made waterfall. There is a little path that allows visitors to step behind the water, so naturally Bob checked it out. Just one of those silly but fun moments.

The Orchid Garden was wonderful. We wandered around and really enjoyed the orchids which were beautiful and growing everywhere in the gardens in which they were displayed. The Celebrity Garden was where the horticulturists breed specialized orchids that are named for various individuals who have some fame or public recognition. Among many others, they had created one for

Queen Elizabeth II, although that one was not on show when we were there. The Mist Garden was quite delightful because every three metres or so a mist of water would spray out intermittently from both sides of the path. It was no doubt meant to benefit the plants, but it was very nice and cooling when following the paths.

After the Orchid Garden, we followed the signs to the Canopy Walk. This is a raised boardwalk through the trees and high above Swan Lake, a body of water initially manmade but now a feature of the environment. Our walk took us down to lake level, and there we saw one single swan in Swan Lake. The bird was duly photographed from many different angles just to prove there was at least one in its namesake lake.

Just walking through the trees was quite the experience as they were huge and towered over us. The groundcover was mainly shade-loving plants and was quite dense. No doubt there were orchids up in the canopy, but not visible to the uninformed.

The Botanical Gardens is an amazing place and would take many visits to explore. We only visited a small and wonderful part of it, and we'd love to go back and spend a lot more time there.

After this lovely visit we went back to the Hop-on Hop-off bus and headed to Orchard Road, one of the main shopping areas. We got off at one of the shopping malls and just wandered around to see what was on offer. By now it was lunchtime, so we found an Italian restaurant then, rested and well fed, made our way to the bus stop. Our bus soon arrived and we were taken to see more parts of the city. The Hop-on Hop-off buses make big circuits around the city, so by choosing from a number of routes you get to see a great deal.

We passed the famous Raffles Hotel, where we hoped to go at a later date, then through the center of town and the business and entertainment areas. To our surprise, the bus stopped at the terminus where we had to change tickets! We never did find out why. We passed the billboard for the Formula One nighttime Grand Prix race, something we have watched on television but never expected to see. We also drove around the central part of the city and the Marina where there are some amazing buildings: the Singapore Skypark, the Singapore Flyer, and the Helix Bridge with its fantastic design. As we drove past, we both agreed that these incredible structures needed a closer look and planned to do this the following day.

LITTLE INDIA

Bob had already seen some of Little India when changing money, so the next day we took the bus and headed off to explore more. The Hop-on Hop-off bus has a fixed route, so we took the long way round—past the Botanical Gardens, down Orchard Road, connecting to another bus on the Hop-on Hop-off system—and finally plunging into the warren of Little India. We

walked down narrow lanes, clustered both sides with booths and stalls selling everything from textiles, spices, clothing, housewares and tourist knick-knacks. Along one of the streets we found the gold merchants so reminiscent of Istanbul, though this time we didn't check out their wares. The smell of the streets was indescribable, a mixture of spices and cooking food, as was the noise and confusion. It was impossible to walk in a straight line. Was this a harbinger of what India will be like? After wandering around for a while, we were ready for a cold drink. We came across a place that could provide us. We went in and thankfully ordered iced cappuccinos. These were quite unlike what we were used to, not as sweet, and ice cubes instead of crushed ice. Different but very good and they sure hit the spot.

Once refreshed, we made our way back to the bus stop. It was very hot and the bus took a while to show up, so we were relieved to get in and cool down as it carried us to our next location, the stadium and the pits of the Formula One race. We found ourselves in the Formula One pit area and imagined how it would look during the racing

We had been told about the views from the Singapore Flyer, the huge Ferris wheel that dominates the Marina, and were looking forward to seeing for ourselves. Unfortunately, it was not to be. It was closed, and we had no idea when it would reopen.

We walked along the path just behind the Flyer and beside the water, which led us down to the Marina and then along to the Helix Bridge. This amazing structure of stainless-steel spans the opening of the Singapore River and is used as a pedestrian bridge and tourist attraction. Throughout the bridge are reflectors, and as you drive across the road bridge beside it you see the reflection of the water. It felt very weird until you understand what is happening.

While walking along the Helix Bridge we could see across the water of the Marina to the Merlion—the Singapore symbol—pouring water out of its mouth. We would see these much closer on an upcoming river trip.

Our return trip bus stop was located beside one the most outrageous buildings in a town famous for its crazy architecture. The Skypark is a huge, ship-shaped platform sitting on top of three towers, 300 metres above the ground and overhanging at both ends. The top surface is covered with grass, trees and other plants, and there are little lakes up there as well. Totally over the top, literally. Unfortunately, we were unable to visit the amazing park, but we could spot it in the distance from Fort Canning Park, which we visited the following day.

That night a Persian restaurant was our choice for supper, and we enjoyed a lovely meal. It was a great way to end a very busy and rewarding day, and sadly we only had one more day here before we headed off to our next port of call, India.

Fort Canning Park

On our last day in Singapore, we stayed close to home and explored the immediate area around the hotel. We took a short stroll beside the river and then made for Fort Canning Park, which is located on a hill surrounded by the city. There are escalators at the foot of the hill to take the less athletic up to the top, and we found this a most civilized arrangement. At the top there was a great cock-a-doodle-doing going on: a beautiful cockerel, who didn't stay around to be admired.

We headed clockwise around the top of the hill, arriving first at a beautiful fountain that celebrates the sacredness of the hill among the Malay people. A natural spring feeds two long pools fed by multiple fountains; it's a lovely restful spot. Another kindly-placed escalator takes you up to the highest level where the British fort is situated. There was an amusing story about the fort: originally conceived for the defence of Singapore in the early 19th century, it turned out that the guns installed didn't have the range to be of any use at all.

We followed signs to the bunker where the capitulation of Singapore to the Japanese was signed in 1942. We would have liked to learn more, but there were no tours available at that time. It was sufficient just to have seen it. Continuing clockwise we came across a cannon aimed outwards from the hill but learned that it had never

been used on this site and was one of two found embedded upright beside the fort's gateway arch. The other cannon was sited a bit further on. In 1903 a lighthouse was installed on the hill, and is now preserved as a historical monument.

One of the ineffective cannon, the lighthouse, and a view of the Skypark.

By this time, the short stroll we had planned had become much longer as we walked right around the park! And as we walked, the heat and humidity rose, so by the end of our walk it was around 30°C and steamy! So much for our nice gentle stroll! Finally, the path took us back to the escalators where we descended to street level and found our way back.

That afternoon was spent organizing our bags and baggage for the next day, a boring but necessary part of our plans. We had decided that for the next leg of travel—to India and Thailand—we would go with much less baggage, so we spent some time sorting out the essentials for the journey, and storing the rest with the hotel. We really appreciated the air-conditioning in our room while completing this necessary chore.

Our last supper of this part of the trip was in a Northern Indian restaurant. We sat outside with Bollywood movies playing on a big screen almost all the time. Fortunately, the volume was low, so it wasn't too intrusive. The dancing and costumes were fantastic and good to watch. What the plot was we never did find out, but that wasn't the point. The food, the reason we were there, was excellent. Bob had a chicken curry, which he found delicious. I had a milder chicken dish, the name of which I cannot remember, not too spicy and very tasty. Rice, pappadums and naan filled out the meal. It was luxurious sitting outside in the warm, but not hot, air and being beside the river as we enjoyed our meal.

After supper we walked alongside the river and finally saw otters hunting for fish. They caught at least one, and two of the others were fighting over the remains. Afterwards they were playing with a beer can which was floating in the water. It was a lot of fun and we spent several minutes just enjoying the spectacle they presented. This was a wonderful way to spend our last day in Singapore before leaving for India.

While we were sorry to be leaving Singapore, but we knew we would be back here after exploring a few places in India and Thailand, and spending time with friends we would meet there.

Chapter Four: Bengaluru and Darjeeling

It was early morning in Singapore and we were waiting for our flight to India, where we would be meeting longtime friends who now live in Bangalore, and doing a little exploring of that huge country. With the limited amount of time, we could be there, we wanted to make the most of it. We felt very fortunate as we settled into our plane seats because we had three for the two of us, as well as reasonable legroom, both of which made the flight more comfortable. We were also given lunch, which was really enjoyable.

Bengaluru

We arrived in Bengaluru in the early stages of the COVID-19 pandemic, and Asian countries were beginning to check travellers for contact with the Wuhan Corona virus, as it was known then. This was January 29th, and not much was known about the virus, but even then, the concern was there.

The immigration process was incredible. After standing in line for half an hour, Bob tried to get us to the front of the line, which helped because then we could go to the 'handicapped' desk. We had filled out multiple forms about our destination, and also answered questions about our health, and then faced them all again at the desk. At the end of it all we discovered that we were at the wrong immigration desk! Fortunately, there were no line-ups at the other desk, as by this time all the passengers had been processed, so our progress was rapid. Now to get our suitcase and clear customs. But before that, our carry-on luggage had to go through security again—we weren't sure why—and then we were released to find our easily spotted pink suitcase.

We found our way to the carousel with the help of a porter. He had a sign embroidered on his shirt that read Paid Porter. This didn't stop him asking for a tip anyway. We had neither dollars nor rupees, and told him so; we were actually being honest. He was upset and we didn't understand why. We later learned that 'Paid Porter' meant he *wasn't* paid! We had to pay! Lost in translation. We then found our way out of the terminal where our friend's son and his driver were waiting to greet us, and so our Indian adventures had begun.

It was an 'interesting' journey. The driving was hectic, irrational and chaotic, with every driver doing their own thing with little or no respect for lane markers or even one-way streets! The combination of people, cars, trucks, motor bikes, and three-wheeled motor rickshaws for passengers and freight was quite the fascination. The din of horns was prodigious, and as everyone was sounding their horn all the time, although the reason for it remained mysterious. And although I had grown up in Trinidad, with its crazy traffic and drivers, this was much more than I had ever seen before! An incredible first experience in India.

While we were on the road, our friend Dave called. He is a teacher, and had taken his class outside into the yard, and pointing his phone at the sky, identified our flight as it passed over, and told his class his 'second parents' were on that plane. The class had all waved at the plane, and we appreciated his thoughtful action.

After a long evening of catching up with all the news, we finally settled down to prepare ourselves for the morning, where we would go shopping, mostly to rectify my lack of wardrobe! Leaving Canada at the start of winter, meant I had neglected to pack many warm weather tops! Winter clothes just don't cut it in India and other warm places, and I had no sandals!

On the way to the shops, we stopped by the Wheel Rail Factory to look at an old steam engine resting quietly in the compound. Then our driver dropped us off in one of the main shopping areas.

Commercial Street was amazing: full of stores of every description; clothing, shoes, decorations, electronics and much, much more. Our first stop was at a Bata shoe store, so reminiscent of my days in Trinidad. The clerks were very attentive and helped me find some nice sandals to replace the ones forgotten at home. It was funny going back to the English sizing after working with North American sizes. It sounds so much better to say your foot is a size six rather than a size nine!

Blouses and tee-shirts were also needed, so when I found a store selling some beautiful items, we went in to try them on. I came out with a lovely one, and our friend was surprised at how relaxed I was in the store. He really didn't expect it, especially when the loafing son/nephew of the owner demanded coffee money, no doubt preying on these foreigners for cash. The poor guy was somewhat disconcerted at my response, which was a firm and polite No. Later on, we came to a larger store, and there I found two very simple tops, which I hoped would carry me through the rest of the trip.

I explained to Dave that both stores were so familiar to me from my childhood that I felt totally at home in them. This was also a surprise for me, because I knew that things would be more exotic in India, compared with shopping in Canada. However, being brought up in Trinidad, so much was similar that it felt normal, and I had just gone with the flow.

Walking down this busy street was fascinating. The need to avoid cars, motorbikes and pedestrians was okay, potholes and very uneven surfaces were expected, but the cows sitting at the side of the road were certainly out of the ordinary. At the end of the street, we came across a vendor on a bicycle that was covered in coconuts. In my youth I had seen many coconut sellers on the street with wagons or trucks, but never on bicycles. That certainly was different!

A cow and coconuts, and the exotic supply of electricity and plumbing to the buildings

After lunch in one of the many cafes, we visited a lovely park and enjoyed walking along the paths in the cool atmosphere the trees created. Some of the trees were ancient, judging by their gnarled trunks and huge canopies spreading over many metres. We also saw what we thought were squirrels. They were about the size of our red squirrels, striped like chipmunks, but moving like squirrels. These were palm squirrels, found in the south of India, as well as other places outside of the sub-continent.

Driving back to our friend's house merely emphasized that driving here is an experience, and this was no exception even though we weren't in rush hour. The roads were crowded and narrow, and the traffic was not always following the rules of the road. Actually, they make their own rules up and everyone seemed to follow them. Motorcycles and scooters were everywhere, weaving in and out of traffic, and finding room for themselves where there seemed to be no room! These two wheeled vehicles are used for so many things: delivering boxes and packages, carrying passengers—maybe one or two or three—food delivery and so on. Some of the riders were carrying things on their backs, others carried items between their legs as well, and even on the handlebars. It was amazing. Frequently you will see a woman in a sari riding sidesaddle on the back of a bike, sometimes but not always, wearing a helmet. Most of the riders seemed to have proper helmets, but often not the passengers.

Mother is sitting side-saddle, and at least the parents have helmets. The child is pretending to steer!

The noise was incredible, with every kind of car, truck, van, and motorbike horn sounding continuously! Our driver had the skill to weave his way through this crazy traffic, and he said that one must be brought up here to be able to drive! Interestingly, the cars are in rather good shape with very few dents or scratches! How more accidents don't occur is a mystery, but it all seems to work.

A quiet evening finished off our first full day in Bengaluru.

THE NANDI HILLS

After all our excitements of the previous day, we slept in, so our planned early morning trip to Nandi Hills was somewhat delayed! After a late breakfast, Dave's driver, took us up to the huge rock outcrops that are known as Nandi Hills. There are several of them jutting out in the middle of a low-lying plain. We were going to the summit of the biggest one, which was crowned by a temple. On the road leading up to the summit there were the remains of a fort and a Sultan's palace. We took a route that passed through a great many villages and farm plots, and we came across very many cows wandering around the land. The cows do belong to individuals, and they know how to get back home in the evening.

In one village we came across a temple that had literally been built into and around a large lump of rock! It

was quite amazing. In many of the fields, upright slabs of granite were used for fencing and fence posts. It would be interesting to know what this granite would cost in Ottawa (we have granite countertops from India in our kitchen) while here is it a very cheap building material!

We came abruptly to the foot of the highest of the Nandi Hills and commenced the climb. It was a very narrow road with numerous tight bends, and it took quite a time to zigzag around before arriving at the parking lot just below the fort entrance. From here we had to walk the rest of the way.

Earlier in the day it would have been possible to drive to the top of the hill, but walking gave us a better overall impression of this fascinating place.

The view from near the top

We followed the road, winding its way around, and then decided to see what the path with steps that paralleled the road would bring. We paused to regain our strength at a charming raised pagoda with a canopy. When we finally arrived at the plateau at the top of the hill, there was a number of small concession stands selling ice cream and drinks. The place was also infested with monkeys, which to our Canadian eyes, were quite exotic. A few minutes after we arrived, we watched a monkey swoop down and grab an ice cream cone right out of a girl's hand! There is no arguing with the monkeys; they will bite and scratch, and that means having to go for rabies shots. If they take your goodies, you wish them luck.

Just reading the ingredients to make sure there's nothing I might react to

Yoga Nandeeshwara Temple

At the summit of the hill a rock shelf sloped slightly upwards, leading to the gateway into the temple precinct. Sitting by the temple door was a lady beside a shoe rack, and once the footwear was removed, she gave you a hand-written number on a card and set the shoes on the rack. We passed through the gate into the temple precinct. The temple was built right onto the sloping surface of the rock, and the pathways were worn smooth by thousands upon thousands of feet. We entered the temple and were greeted by the Hindu priest, who showed us around the dim interior. Before our little tour began, we placed some money on a collection plate, and he blessed us with a dab of ash on our foreheads. He told us that the temple was 600 years old and showed us the statues of the deities in various rooms. We were shown around as tourists, but a couple were there for the religious experience and were praying to all the deities. It was an honour to be in this special place. My overwhelming feeling while walking around was that of serenity. The temple had a very calming feeling about it, which was quite wonderful. After looking around and appreciating this special building we left and were grateful for the brief time had we spent there.

The temple precinct and the carvings of Ganesha that flank the steps

We collected our shoes, gave the lady a little money, and walked up to the concessions. We found one place that had a cage built around the eating area. So, in we went and bought some ice creams. We were in the cage and the monkeys were looking in! No doubt they were feeling frustrated because they couldn't get to our ice creams, while we felt like the specimens in the cage. A couple of them tried to get through the door but were shooed away. There was one mother with the baby clinging on to her belly. It really was quite something to see.

On our walk back down to the car, we paid more attention to the ancient walls. There are two sets of defensive walls right around the hill: the inner wall, which we believe was the original, and the outer one that was built later, probably as an extra defensive line. We were also able to see some of the remains of other buildings on this site, and wondered what they could tell us about the people who lived there so long ago. Nandi Hills was an amazing place to visit, with the monkeys and the temple as the highlights.

This was our last day in Bengaluru, so to celebrate we all went out for supper at the Orchid Garden, a lovely restaurant nearby. Then, after talking forever through the evening, it was time to get ready to leave. We were heading off to Kolkata and further adventures in this incredible country.

Passing Through Kolkata

The next day we flew into Kolkata, and were met by the Marriot limousine and driven to the hotel through the chaos that is Indian roads. Since we had been in India, we had been totally overwhelmed with people offering to do things for us. It is quite something. The hotel itself was unbelievable, with over-the-top decoration and a luxurious room. You could hold a dance in there. Although we were just here for one night before went on to Darjeeling, we would be coming back after our tour, and then we would be able to explore some small part of this exciting city.

Right from the beginning of our plans for this trip, Darjeeling was at the top of our list. As a small boy Bob had read about the Darjeeling Himalaya Railway and had dreamed of riding on it one day. Now the time had finally come. Early the next morning we were picked up at our hotel by the Apollo Travel tour company driver and taken to the airport for our flight to Bagdogra, the jumping off point for this part of our trip. The drive was less crazy than usual, as it was fairly early on Sunday morning.

When we arrived at the airport the fun started. We had to show our tickets to an armed guard before entering the terminal. Then our suitcase had to be screened and passed before we could check in. Once the appropriate sticky tag was applied to the lock on the case, we were permitted to check in and drop off our bag. Now it was our turn for security. In every airport I had been in the line-up for security has been long, and this was no exception. The line was moving well until a group of people pushed in a little way ahead of us! Much shouting and gesticulating ensued by those displaced, but to no avail. The intruders said they were in the line and, of course, having forced their way in, they were! The people behind them were not happy, and let their feelings be known. It didn't quite get physical.

It was finally our turn with the usual requirements: off came the belts, out came all the electronics, but the shoes stayed on. Bob went through the screening arch with no problem. I was stopped and directed to the other side of the room. Ladies had their own screening behind curtains, so I had to join that queue. This line was much quicker, which I appreciated. When I came out, I couldn't find my belt because it had got stuck in the conveyor of the screening machine! Fortunately, Bob spotted it and the personnel released it, so my jeans were once more held up properly.

Even though we were early, we made our way to the gate, just to find out where it was. Then went to the priority lounge where we relaxed with some tea, returning just before boarding. The area was crowded, hot and noisy, with everyone talking at the top of their lungs, children all over the place, with the line-up to board wending its way all through the area. We waited patiently to be boarded, only to find airport buses lining up to take passengers to the plane. It took me back many years, before the time of jetways when only first-class passengers had them, and local flights didn't need them. When we arrived at the plane, instead of stairs there were gentle ramps, which we considered very civilized. Once on the plane we found we were seated in the emergency exit row, so we had plenty of legroom. Our seatmate was a lovely lady from South Africa who was leading a tour group. The tours were designed to take people out of their comfort zone and give them challenging experiences. We talked about our trip among many other things, which made the flight to Bagdogra seem to go much faster than they normally do.

BAGDOGRA TO DARJEELING

Once we had landed and acquired our luggage, we were met by Kiran our guide, who was waiting for us with his sign. He quickly located our luggage, took us to the car and introduced us to Suren, the driver. We were happy to learn we were the only tourists on this tour, so Kiran and the driver would be with us for the whole time. It was a very smooth and easy start to the tour.

The drive from Bagdogra up to Darjeeling is beyond spectacular, although the first 20 or so kilometers pass through villages on the plain that sort of blend into each other. Driving through one village we passed an accident. A cow had been hit by something, not sure what, but I did see a motor scooter lying on its side. The cow did not look healthy, but it was touching to see someone stroking her neck and talking to her.

When the road turns off the plain and starts to climb, it's a whole different story. It zigzags all the way up, clinging to the sides of the hills,

passing buildings perched on the very edges of precipices, cantilevered out and built on piles. We've been on many narrow mountain roads over the years, but none have gone on for so long and so unrelentingly. We stopped for a rest and a snack of Darjeeling tea and local dumplings about halfway up.

Soon after our break, the road met the Darjeeling Himalaya Railway tracks and from there on rails and road shared the right of way. We crossed and recrossed the tracks countless times, and it was curious to see how the railway line ran through the villages and towns, right up against shopfronts and houses. We thought the train whistle must get a lot of use as it passes by. About eight kilometers from Darjeeling, we came to Ghum, and encountered our first steam train. We were both very excited, as we were going to be riding on it the next day. Closer to Darjeeling we passed the train terminus where three little blue engines were parked.

(Above) Like all buildings in Darjeeling the Elgin Hotel is perched on the side of a hill. There are very few level places

(Right) The furnishing is in the style of the bygone days of the Raj, with heavy ornate furniture, thick carpeting, and shelves of knick-knacks

The staff greeted us by placing light silken scarves around our necks, and then inviting us to sit down for high tea; a light black tea served without milk, and a wide range of cookies on a three-tier rack. It was so old-world we could hardly believe it. Dinner that night had all the ceremony one would expect of a century ago. The food was excellent, the waiters swooped at every pause, and we luxuriated in the atmosphere. The daytime temperature was pleasant, but it did get chilly at night, so the lounge and other public areas had coal fires. Later, when we climbed into bed, we found hot water bottles had already been inserted between the sheets, and we slid into a warm, welcoming place.

THE DARJEELING HIMALAYA RAILWAY

We woke up the next morning very excited, because today we would ride on the toy train, the Darjeeling Himalaya Railway. The breakfast room was empty except for one guy who appeared to be alone. We invited him over to our table and had a very nice conversation. He was an ophthalmology student who had been doing PhD research in Nepal on a particular fugal eye infection, and would complete the work in Kenya. We exchanged quite a few similar stories as he was studying at the London School of Hygiene and Tropical Medicine, where my father had studied, and Bob had worked at the School of Pharmacy. One of those intriguing coincidences that always seem to be more frequent than they should be. He had also booked a ride on the toy train, so we told him we'd probably see him there.

After breakfast we headed to the station for our ride on the Darjeeling Himalaya Railway. It is amazing to think that the British could conceive of running a two-foot gauge railway up here, let alone carrying it off. Construction was started in 1850 and completed 31 years later. It is now, quite justifiably, designated as a World Heritage Site.

The train ride started in Darjeeling and finished in Ghum—a distance of about eight kilometers—with a stop halfway at the Batasia Loop where we would visit a memorial to World War II Gurkhas. Kiran met us at the hotel and we drove down to the station where we found our train waiting.

Departure was for 9:30 but we were told the train would follow Darjeeling time; in other words, when it was good and ready. We had lots of time to examine the locomotives and rolling stock, and peer into one of the classic passenger cars, which had beautiful wooden fittings and luxurious upholstery. One engine was already in steam on a siding next to the station, and another was in the maintenance shed across the road, along with three of its buddies.

Examining the engines close-up was to marvel at the ancient technology, still functioning after 140 years. These engines are not in showroom condition: they are battered and dirty, their blue paint is overlaid with smoke stains and oil, and there is much evidence of repair and maintenance. The copper and brass fittings are well tarnished and dented. All this, of course, lends to the engines' charm and appeal. The smell of burnt coal and hot oil was fabulous; it could be bottled and sold for a fortune (but perhaps only to steam train nuts).

Our train comprised just two carriages. A conductor with a seating plan on a clipboard was directing everyone to their allotted seats. We saw our companion from breakfast, who was in the first carriage, while we would be in the back of other, right at the rear of the train. Travelling with us was a very excited group from Taiwan. They were not alone in their excitement, as we too were excited and could hardly wait for the train to start.

Finally, after much whistling and flag waving from the man on the platform, and answering shrieks from the engine, the train started forward with a jerk accompanied by a thunderous slipping of wheels as the engine gained traction. The noise of the exhaust beats coupled with the rumble of the carriages was deafening. This railway passes right through the towns and villages on the route, often sharing the road with the traffic and weaving across from side to side. 'Right through' means passing by houses, shops, market stalls and kiosks so close that you could literally reach out from your window and steal things off the shelves. And because the streets are so narrow, the incredible din is magnified and reverberates off the walls. And yes, the whistle gets a great workout travelling through these very tight spaces. It was an amazing, all-senses experience.

(Above) The Gurkha War Memorial at Batasia Loop
(Right) Traffic waits while the train occupies the roadway

The stop at Batasia Loop

The Batasia Loop stop was for 10 minutes to stretch our legs and examine the Gurkha war memorial, which was very simple and tastefully done. The memorial and its surrounding gardens are laid out in a circle, which is defined by the loop of the track. From here the railway must gain considerable elevation, and these loops are a very simple way of doing this in a tight space. It is only with narrow gauge tracks that this can be done effectively.

Along the sides of the track vendors—mostly women—had laid out all manner of textile products, from raw cloth to finished garments. There were also numerous sellers of all kinds of tourist trinkets, snacks and drinks. After 10 minutes of visiting, several blasts of the whistle made it clear that passengers should board, and soon we were off again. As we gained speed, we completed the loop, passed over a bridge and looked down on the tracks below. The locomotive laboured mightily over this final climbing stretch, even with only two carriages, so it would probably be necessary to double-head heavier trains. We steamed into Ghum station, the highest railway station in India at 2258m above sea level, and when built was the highest in the world. We were delighted with the experience, which far exceeded expectations in many ways, but somewhat sad that the experience, so long awaited, was now in the past. But we still have our memories of this unique train ride.

TIGER HILL

After our wonderful train ride, we were driven to Tiger Hill, one of the best places to see the Himalayas from Darjeeling. The drive took us through a wildlife sanctuary where the Red Panda is protected. This panda is native to the eastern Himalayas and southwestern China. It is listed as an endangered species because the wild population is thought to be fewer the 10,000 animals. Its major food source is bamboo, which is plentiful in this sanctuary. The pandas are rarely seen as the noise of the road keeps them away, which is a good thing for an endangered species.

The road twists and turns it way up the hill through an increasing numbers of hairpin bends. As you get near the top of the hill, Buddhist prayer flags are seen in ever-increasing numbers, crossing and re-crossing the road on lines. Other flags have been hung from the trees alongside the road. It was clear that a few were very old, while others were fairly fresh and been installed quite recently.

Even with Photoshop haze reduction, this was the best we could do. The most prominent peak in this view is Kangchenjunga, third highest in the world after Everest and K-2

There were many cars and visitors at the summit. Coming up in the late morning it was not too busy, but our guide told us that in the early morning on a clear day there could be over 300 hundred people waiting for the sunrise, and they would all be struggling and pushing for the best viewing spot. So, we were glad we had chosen to come later.

It was quite hazy, so the Himalayas were obscured for most of the time. At one point we could see the peaks very faintly through the intervening cloud. Our pictures were disappointing as the mountains were just too far away and the haze too thick. However, we know we have actually seen the Himalayas.

As a point of interest, our guide told us there are no tigers on Tiger Hill. Rather, it was named after a British Battalion called the Tigers, who were posted there in the early 20th century.

THE YIGA CHEOLING MONASTERY

A Buddhist monastery was next on our tour guide's list. The Yiga Cheoling Monastery was established in 1850 and is the oldest Buddhist establishment in Darjeeling. This monastery was dedicated to the Future Buddha; the spiritual leader who was predicted to return to earth. Unlike the purer Buddhist sects in

Nepal and Bhutan, the believers here combine many elements of Hinduism into their decorations, so we were told we would see some very elaborate murals and sculptures. After the necessary removal of our shoes, we were shown in and instructed to follow a path around the building in a clockwise direction. Going the other way would be bad luck, and the same applies to rotating the prayer wheels. Our guide told us that prayer wheels were invented only 100 or so years ago as a way of ensuring that the illiterate could pray. The prayers are written on the outside so the rotation gives the impression of reading from left to right.

The monastery, the Future Buddha, and a large metal prayer wheel

The Future Buddha was a huge sculpture dominating the inner chamber, reaching up to the ceiling, and brightly decorated with paint, gold and fabrics. The murals were also produced in fantastic colours and depicted the life of the Buddha and many stories and myths associated with him. Outside, with shoes thankfully back on very cold feet, we examined two enormous prayer wheels, on either side of the door. They were drums of metal perhaps six feet in diameter and about twelve high, with pivots and bearings at top and bottom. They would be heavy to move, but we couldn't see any driving mechanism that might make praying easier.

It was a really informative first learning opportunity about Buddhism, and some of the basic teachings of the Buddha.

THE PADMAJA NAIDU HIMALAYAN ZOOLOGICAL PARK

After a very welcome cup of tea, we left the monastery and were driven to the Padmaja Naidu Himalayan Zoological Park. The zoo is built on the side of the hill—like virtually everything else in Darjeeling—so the animal enclosures are large and slope downhill. As you go up the pathway you look down on the animals on one side and look up to them on the other side. The return path is at a higher level, so you just look down. It seems an unusual way of building a zoo, but when all you have is the side of a mountain, you make it work. We enjoyed seeing the animals, but our main goal was the Himalaya Mountaineering Institute, and we had to pass by the animals first to get there.

THE HIMALAYA MOUNTAINEERING INSTITUTE

The institute is funded and run by the military, which seemed a bit odd to us. However, we learned that this location is close to where India borders China, among several other countries, so a military presence requires training in the skills to work in these high and difficult areas. To emphasise the mountaineering theme, outside the building there are various activities for kids to try, including climbing, swinging, and rope ladders. We saw a couple of kids being kitted out for a very shallow zip-line. They looked happy to be trying this out. We climbed up stairs to the museum, which documents the history of the conquest of Mount Everest.

This was a very well documented series of exhibits, outlining the attempts at climbing the mountain and the clothes and equipment the mountaineers used. The clothes from the early days didn't look as if they would protect the climbers much, and the equipment was primitive, but as mountaineering progressed the clothing improved in both warmth and practicality. Some of the clothes, tents and sleeping bags in the later exhibits could have come from any major outfitting store in North America. Development of the equipment over the period showed how it had become more practical and useful, and stronger and lighter.

A relief map of the Himalayas was incredible; a scale diorama of the entire range, with the most well-known mountains identified. Seeing the extent of the map made us realize just how big this chain of mountains really is. I was surprised to see what a huge area they covered and the number of mountains in the entire chain. I had never realized the extent of them. The display label identified the eight highest peaks, all over 8,000 metres, including Everest, K2 and Kangchenjunga, all of which are in India.

Tenzing Norgay, the first man to summit Everest, is buried in the precincts of the institute in a beautiful memorial. Edmund Hillary was initially given credit for being first to the summit, and it was only after both men had passed away that the record was set straight and Tenzing finally received this honour.

Tea Tasting

Our last port of call on this busy and fascinating day, was small tea store in Chaulk Bazaar where we sat down for a formal tea tasting! This was similar to the wine tastings we have attended; you are given a series of teas to taste and judge. We had seven teas ranged in glasses in front of us: a spring Darjeeling, a middle Darjeeling, a late Darjeeling, a green tea, a white tea and a couple of other ones.

Each of them had a unique character: some tasted drier than others, the green tea had a grassy taste, which we didn't find pleasant, and others just weren't right for our taste. In the end we bought two of the seven varieties: Darjeeling white tea and Spring Romance, an organic Darjeeling Tea. They were vacuum packed so they would last until we got home to enjoy them. This was our first souvenir of this extensive trip. No doubt there will be others, but we would have to wait and see because space was at a minimum.

After the tea tasting, we had some time to ourselves, so our first stop was Oxford Bookstore, which had been recommended by our friends. We wandered around and Bob found a map of India, which made him very happy. He always enjoys reading maps and finding out exactly where he is in the world. After that we simply walked around the Chauk Bazaar Plaza, peeping into the many stalls and shops, before heading home to the hotel and afternoon tea.

This had been a very long and full day, so it was time to rest and think about all we had seen. Tomorrow we would head to Gangtok over the border in Sikkim.

Chapter Five: Gangtok

The day started nicely with chance encounters over breakfast. We had noticed the young lady having dinner by herself the previous evening, and wondered if we should have invited her to our table. So, this morning we did. She was a pediatric neurosurgeon from Brazil attending a conference in Kolkata, and rather than attend the tours laid on by the organizers, she decided to come to Darjeeling. We had a lovely talk about her work and family, then chatted about our travels and our careers. Child-protection social work moved into museum conservation, at which point a lady at another table came over. She couldn't help overhearing our conversation and after being assured that Bob had worked in the museum field, she wondered if he had heard of her father-in-law who had just retired from a career in paintings restoration at the Kolkata Museum. Bob knew of him and remembered that he had organized a conference in Kolkata for the International Institute for Conservation. It is indeed a small world.

Kiran called for us at 10:00, and we headed off to Gangtok. It was a clear day, so the Himalayas were visible, which gave us the opportunity to see them again. We were surprised to see the mountains soaring much higher above the horizon than we had thought they would be, even at this distance. We

needed to look up to them, even though they were still far away. As we drove down the road out of Darjeeling, we had another chance to see the little train, as it had just stopped for water.

We turned off the main road at Ghum and started on the windiest, zigzagiest, hairpiniest road we could imagine, surpassing the road up from Siliguri in its length. We stopped a little below Tiger Hill—we could see the antenna and viewing structure up on the ridge—and had another view of the Himalayas. This was the last we would see of them because the air began to get really hazy, although the sun still shone. We passed through innumerable small villages, each with their amazingly coloured and decorated houses and shops. No matter how humble the building was, the owners took great trouble in making it look its best. The yellows, violets, blues and pinks were like nothing we see at home, although some Newfoundland villages could give them a run for their money.

(Left) We rarely saw clear skies on this leg of the journey, so the glimpses we had had of the Himalayas would not be repeated

(Below) A colourful street scene on the road to Sikkim

A large part of this drive was through forests of tall pine. These are not native to this part of India, but a few were brought here from Japan by the British for making tea chests. It turned out that tea shipped in pine chests very soon began to taste like pine, so this particular idea was a failure. The pine trees didn't know this, and so proceeded to spread in every direction. The local people now make their houses out of this plentiful and readily available wood.

After what seemed an age, we came to a stop at a little tea plantation beside the road. We walked among the bushes and examined the two kinds of tea they were growing there: a small-leafed Chinese variety and a larger leafed Indian one. Only the greenest of the top leaves, we were told, were harvested (we could see the cut ends) and the rest of the leaves were left to support the bush. White tea, the most expensive, is taken from the thin pointed shoot in the centre of a leaf bunch. Some of the bushes had yellow and white flowers, and lots also had round white buds.

After examining the tea, we crossed the road to a tiny teashop, and our guide brought us tea and cookies as we sat for a peaceful interlude in the company of a lovely little puppy who was tied to our bench. He loved the cookies and kept asking for more!

Rushes laid out to protect the tea bushes, and a close-up of tea leaves

Then it was back on the road, heading down into the valley of the Teesta River, which we would eventually cross into Sikkim. As the road descended into the valley it passed through teak forests. This wood is excellent for making furniture and is also used in boat- and ship-building because of its resistance to rotting. The sides of the road were populated by groups of monkeys who appeared to favour this kind of forest. They seemed not to be worried by the traffic, and just sat on the walls and fences beside the road, minding their own business.

As we came close to Rangpo, where we would cross the border from Punjab into Sikkim, there came a slight hiccup: a traffic jam. It started about three or four kilometres before Rangpo, and everyone was travelling at a snail's pace. Our tour guide could see no reason for it, so our driver asked a passer-by, who told us it was the sixth anniversary of the SKM Front, the political party presently in power, and thus a day of celebration. Now we understood why the cars, trucks and motorbikes were all dressed with flags and banners. The sides of the road were similarly decorated to celebrate this important day.

As we slowly approached Rangpo, we began to come across groups of people walking along beside the road, as well as countless taxis parked on either side of this rather narrow way. What with the people and the parked cars, the driving was horrendous. Our driver Suren had to avoid the people, the motor bikes, the cars, trucks, and buses coming towards him, all going slowly but filling the road. It really was a mess, but everybody appeared happy, they were having a good time, and we were happy to be there.

The crowd by this time was huge, and as we drove into the town, we were going so slowly we were able to take any pictures we wanted, both of people and places, without the need for the driver to slow down! At times he was almost at a full stop already. At one place we passed an egg seller, and we couldn't remember when we had ever seen so many eggs!

Finally, our driver found his way across the river into the town, and through to the police station/border post. It is necessary for all travellers to Sikkim to pass border clearance because there is increased vigilance and military presence this close to the borders of Nepal and China.

The traffic chaos affected everything, including the police station where the parking was a disaster. The official parking lot was utterly chaotic, but our driver was able to manoeuvre the car into a very tight spot! Once parked, Kiran took us to the official building through a melee of cars, and one careless driver actually banged the fender of his car into Bob's wrist. He shook it off and no harm was done, thank goodness. We were left in what we believed was the Sikkim Police mess hall, while Kiran sorted out all the official paperwork for us to legally enter this part of India. We sat in the mess hall with a cup of tea and waited for Kiran to return with all the paperwork. Formalities concluded it was now time to join in the ever-increasing traffic jam as we made our way to Gangtok!

The traffic decreased as we drove further along the road and, finally, after what seemed ages, we were out of it and travelling easily toward the city of Gangtok. We climbed into the mountains and then had to descend toward the Teesta River and cross over it again before climbing back up. As always on these mountain roads hairpin bends were quite something, even more extreme than the ones we had seen earlier in the day.

Finally, we drove through a busy shopping area, thinking we were close to our destination, but no, it was further on again. Gangtok is a very spread-out town, several kilometres long and hugging the sides of the hills. Sikkim seems not to have flat spot anywhere and the house builders have either burrowed into the sides of the hills—very labour-intensive and costly—or built out on piles and cantilevers. Either way, the creativity and engineering are quite impressive.

Equally impressive is the electrical, plumbing, and telephone distribution; apparently chaotic yet clearly functional

At last, we turned into a narrow road and came to the gates to the Nor-Khill Hotel. These gates were similar to those at the hotel in Darjeeling, probably because this was one of the same chain. The building was apparently a palace in the 19th century, and on entering we could well believe it. We were welcomed into a luxurious common room, given the traditional scarf and a glass of juice, and thankfully made our way up to our room.

The hotel had the same 19th century elegance we had enjoyed in Darjeeling

Dinner was as luxurious and beautifully served as the hotel in Darjeeling. Over our meal we got talking to a lady at the next table. She was visiting India for the first time in 40 years, having stopped over back then from her first job as an airline hostess with BOAC. We exchanged stories and talked over a wide range of topics. We learned that she was from Chichester—not far from where Bob's mum had lived—and had worked at the Downlands Museum close by. She preferred to leave her workaholic husband at home and travel by herself. A very nice companion to share supper with, and a peaceful end to a very interesting day's travel.

RUMTEK MONASTERY

Our visit to the Rumtek Monastery promised to be interesting because it is close to the border with China. The monastery is high on a hill opposite Gangtok, so the drive meant going right the way through Gangtok, down to the bottom of the valley, and right the way up the other side. It took the longest time to get out of Gangtok itself because it winds around the side of the hills. Like all the roads we have been on, it zigzags with scarcely any straight sections. In two places there were road works that slowed us down;

one where a bridge was being replaced and another where resurfacing was being done. The drive over the temporary road of rocks and gravel reminded us of driving in Labrador. We passed rice irrigation terraces on the sides of the hills, and tea plantations, all of which were for local consumption.

Rumtek Monastery was built in the 1960s after China had annexed Tibet. The Black Hat sect of Buddhists from Tibet brought all their ceremonial materials to Sikkim and raised money for a new building. The monastery was in need of a new hereditary Lama, and in the process of selecting one, the Sikkim faction and the Tibet faction each came up with their own candidate, and this resulted in violence. The army was called in, and there is still a very heavy military presence around the monastery to make sure that peace is kept until the situation is sorted out. And there we were thinking how peaceful Buddhism was supposed to be! But, far from being a religious issue, the conflict actually revolves around a fund of 1.5 billion dollars that the monastery holds!

We arrived at the foot of the hill and stopped at a military checkpoint to have our passports examined. The road up to the monastery is very long and very steep, and it is barred to anything but official motor vehicles. However, our guide obtained permission from the guards to have Suren drive us up. We passed many tourists labouring up the hill, including the South African lady we had met on the plane to Bagdogra. We got out of the car at the top, entered the courtyard and were amazed at the decoration of the temple. It was elaborately covered with carvings and architectural elements, all gorgeously painted in multiple colours with lots of gilding. We had to take our shoes off before entering, of course. Inside, the decoration was equally rich, with sculptures paintings and textiles. The walls were furnished with hundreds of cubbyholes that contained the writings of Buddha and later

commentaries, and 1,000 identical brass statuettes. In front of the huge seated Buddha statue was a picture of the late lama, the 13th in line of this sect.

After leaving the temple, we climbed the stairs to a gallery around the courtyard that offered a great view over the area. We met our South African friend again, and she told us that she had mentioned us to her travelling companions, so we appeared to have acquired some kind of fame. It was fun chatting with her, and following the required photo session, we exchanged email addresses and promised to be in touch. Sometimes simply striking up conversations with people is a very rewarding experience.

One of the monks graciously allowed himself to be photographed with the monastery's cat. We decided to walk back down the steep hill, rather than have the car come up for us, and a very steep hill it was! We settled thankfully in a teahouse and enjoyed cups of tea with a very pleasant, almost peppery spicing.

SIKKIM RESEARCH INSTITUTE OF TIBETOLOGY

After the visit to the temple, it was back down the mountain, with its many rice terraces. We made our way to the Sikkim Research Institute of Tibetology, which was founded in 1957 and where the 14th Dalai Lama had placed the foundation stone on February 10th of that year. It was formally opened on October 1st, 1958 by Pandit Jawaharlal Nehru, Prime Minister of India.

The Research and Educational areas of the Institute are not open to the public, but the museum welcomes visitors, although no photography is allowed. Once inside the building we found a wonderful depiction of the origins of Buddhism. Moving clockwise to enhance positive energy, you come upon a range of bronze statues depicting the Buddha. A large statue of the Buddha is placed in the centre of the museum, so that it is the first thing a visitor would see on entering the building. As you continue round there are 14 wonderful silk panels with painted pictures telling the story of the Buddha from his conception to his enlightenment. To help those who do not know the story of the Buddha, there are very helpful labels explaining the panels.

The many religious artifacts used in the temple ceremonies had informative display labels explaining their function. There were further silk

panels telling the story of the followers of Buddha and of their struggles to reach enlightenment. The workmanship in these panels was quite wonderful, both as works of art and as means of teaching others.

One very special exhibit was of the handmade paper and printing blocks for the words and teachings of the Buddha from much earlier times. Seeing the bronze blocks of text for printing, which have been passed down for so many years, was a reminder of just how long people have been following the teachings of the Buddha.

Gangtok Stupa

This very large stupa was our next stop. We learned that a stupa is a monument with a spire and its function is to ward off all the bad karma of an area. This one was huge and loomed above us as we walked up the very steep road. The stupa is about 30 feet high and sits on a pedestal in the middle

of an open square, with the dormitories of the monks all round it. The wall surrounding the stupa was lined with dozens of drum-shaped prayer wheels painted in dark red with gold lettering, which everyone was allowed to turn and pray. In one place a monk was busy repainting the lettering on some of the drums as it becomes worn away as people turn the drums by hand. At one side of the precinct was a building with curious smoke stains on its outside. Peeping in through the windows we could watch monks preparing thousands of votive candles, cleaning little blackened bronze cups, pouring in molten ghee, and then inserting pointed cotton wicks ready for the faithful to light and pray, for a fee.

ARTS AND CRAFTS SCHOOL

In 1959 the American wife of the Crown Prince of Sikkim dedicated the Arts and Crafts building, a school for the teaching of local arts and crafts to young women in the area. The skills they learned at the school gave them opportunities to make positive changes in their lives. Some of the graduates of the program remained there to teach, while others would return to their villages to pass on their skills in their locality. Others were able to sell their work in local markets and stores. Inside the market building we got a good idea of some of the wonderful work. Beautifully crafted stuffed animals of all sizes, crocheted articles of clothing, lovely dresses, and finely made carpets were some of the first things we saw. As we wandered through the three rooms, we came across carved and painted boxes and other wooden items, handmade paper, and diaries and notebooks made from it. There was also a poster showing bottled preserves for sale, and a big table of the preserves themselves.

We were most impressed, but not surprised by the quality of the work. It was a bit disappointing because there were things I would loved to have bought and brought back to Canada. However, because we were travelling, we really couldn't take advantage of the offerings of this very special market.

This teaching of crafts to the young reminded us that, throughout our time in this region, we had frequently seen children in school uniforms on their way to and from school. Kiran mentioned the importance of schooling, and told us of the high literacy rate here, which averaged 77% in 2017-18.

FLORAL GREENHOUSES

We finished the day quietly with a visit to a floral exhibition in a large roofed-over space. This exhibition comprised flowers native to Sikkim at this time of the year. We followed a sinuous path through the exhibits, delighted with the colours and variety. There was a great sweep of bromeliads with dark green leaves and red centres, peonies, and many varieties of orchid.

Outside the exhibition space there was little boutique that sold packages of seeds, some of which it would have been nice to buy. Although tempting, it would not be sensible to try bringing seeds back to Canada, where they might be confiscated at the border, in case they came into competition with our native plants.

Chapter Six: Return to Kolkata

The following morning we would return south to Kolkata. We left early, bringing a breakfast package prepared by hotel staff. The first part of our journey was the reverse of our outward journey, clearing the checkpoint at Rangpo and crossing the Teesta back into West Bengal. This time we noticed the route was populated by monkeys, sitting on the roadside barriers by the dozens. We assumed that the parade we had come across on our way up had frightened them off. The route followed the river until we recrossed it, and then we branched off in the direction of Siliguri. Much to our surprise, our guide pointed out the multitude of pharmaceutical factories that occupied this area of the Teesta valley. Drugs are a major export industry, and it made us wonder how many of the medications we use here in Canada were produced on the banks of the Teesta River.

After a long drive down the mountains, we arrived in the plains, and with the flat country came the traffic jams. Our driver was superb, and we made it to the airport in Bagdogra in plenty of time for our flight. We said goodbye to Kiran and Suren and thanked them for all they had done. It had been a wonderful experience and made better by these two helpful and accommodating people.

Return to Kolkata

Our flight and all the formalities were both quick and efficient, likely because Bagdogra is a small airport, with fewer flights than many. After an uneventful flight we collected our luggage and made our way out to where the driver from Apollo Travel was waiting for us. Then the fun began. We had become a little familiar with the route to our hotel, and we had clearly passed the Marriott when the driver handed Bob the phone. The hotel was enquiring at what time we wanted the car for the airport tomorrow! Bob was surprised at this question and mentioned that we were not leaving for some days, and was promptly told we had no booking beyond today. This was odd, since we had a booking at our hotel, the Marriot. Finally, it all came clear. The package tour we had booked also included a night in Kolkata at a hotel they had booked. So, we were heading to the Peerless Inn for our final night of the tour.

This was an 'interesting' experience. The hotel lived up to its name: Peerless, but not in a positive way! On arrival at the hotel, we were given milky chai, while we waited to find out where we would be sleeping that night. The wait for our room seemed endless, and we were falling asleep sitting in our chairs! Finally, we were conducted to our room in the hotel annex, up one elevator, across a bridge and down another, far away from everything!

We flopped down thankfully while the porter stood with an obvious expression of expectation. Sadly, we didn't have any small bills, so he had to go away empty handed.

While relaxing we thought how nice it would be to watch TV. No such luck, we couldn't find the news channel we wanted, neither could the multiple technicians who were sent to help us when we called. To a man, they did exactly same things we had done, with the same results. The classical definition of insanity. So, no relaxing TV for us.

We ordered room service for supper, a tomato soup, and a variety of breads. The soup was very tasty and, like most dishes, had a little peppery spice added to it. Then we thought it would be nice to get a hot drink from the little stand in the foyer. Then came the most farcical of farces; Bob went down and asked for two cups of tea. The server behind the counter didn't seem to know what to do and he disappeared into the bar across the hall. Five minutes later he came back with another man who asked Bob if he wanted tea. Yes, Bob answered, he did. A third guy came along at this point, but he seemed to be just standing around and watching. One cup of tea was duly made, Bob insisting on them using just a little cold milk instead of the steamed milk that was about to be added. Was that all? No, two cups please. Another cup was made, a tray was brought out and some biscuits added. Now was the time to pay. They wanted to add it the room bill, but Bob wanted to pay cash because our room was all paid for. It was not possible to come to any agreement, so a managing-type man was called over (the fourth employee on the great tea project). Bob insisted on paying cash; the man insisted that it must be charged to the room. This went on for some time until Bob sort of lost his cool a bit and said that while this argument was in progress the tea was now getting cold. No problem there; they put the cups under the cappuccino spout and roared steam into them. Finally, an agreement was made that if one of the servers carried the tray to our room, we could pay him with cash. So off they went, Bob holding open doors while the server insisted that he go first—a very awkward protocol with spring-loaded double doors—then up one elevator, across the bridge and down another. The tea was very welcome, made even more refreshing by the rigmarole attendant on its production!

We had had a wonderful time in the north of India, with so many memories and experiences, and while thinking about them and wondering what we would see in the next few days, we gladly went to bed, looking forward to what the future would bring.

After our interesting sojourn at the Peerless we made our way back to the Marriot where we were welcomed to our room, in which we would stay for the next couple of days. One of our first tasks was the laundry, a chore that is not left behind when you travel. Fortunately, we were able to pass this on to the much-appreciated hotel laundry service, and the reason this mundane chore is mention in this book relates to the quality of the experience. Our laundry came back later that day in two leather-bound boxes, with each item wrapped in thin tissue paper. Once the tissue was laid back, the neatly folded laundry was revealed. Each shirt had a cardboard insert and a paper binding tape, the underwear was impossibly flat and even, and the socks were all laid out in rows like soldiers on parade. Numbers on fabric tags were attached to each item with the tiniest safety pins we had ever seen, and which we were still discovering weeks later.

Once this delightful chore was completed, the next was charging up all the electronics. We came well prepared for the variety of electrical outlets and voltages we would encounter, so we plugged every device in. Next, we needed to charge ourselves. A light lunch in the hotel was a wonderful way to relax but later in the afternoon a waiter appeared at our door with a tray of cheese, crackers, cake and fruit, and an anonymous blue drink. It was all part of the service, and we really appreciated it. All in all, a very relaxing, rejuvenating, amusing and gastronomic day.

Exploring Kolkata

We set out next morning armed with a map from the concierge, who also called a taxi for us. We had planned to see the planetarium and the gardens around the Victoria Museum, but found both of them closed. We spotted the cathedral across the other side of the road so we aimed ourselves there. This sounds simpler than it was! Crossing a road in Kolkata, and any other busy place in India, is an adventure. At first it appears to be a perilous task, until you realize that nobody actually wants to run into you because it would involve all sorts of nuisance. Even so, for the beginner road-crosser it's best to watch what everybody else does and follow them. Traffic lights will not help you to make decisions! We quickly learned how to cross these very busy roads safely, so by the time we left Kolkata we had become experts in the art!

St Paul's Cathedral

Once over the road, we approached the cathedral along a drive that led into a square decorated with flower beds. The traffic noise thankfully diminished as we walked in, and we thought the air quality had improved a little, but that may have been imaginary! The cornerstone of St Paul's Cathedral was laid in 1839, and the building was completed in 1847. It is built in the gothic revival style with some modern elements. In 1897 it suffered damage and needed to be refurbished, then in 1934 a devastating earthquake rocked Kolkata, and the steeple tower fell. It was rebuilt in the style of the central Bell Harry tower of Canterbury Cathedral. The interior of the cathedral is unlike the typical layout because there are no aisles, and the nave is vaulted right across with steel arches. It makes for a very impressive space.

What most drew our attention were the commemorative plaques to those who had given their lives for the British Empire. Prominent among the plaques were ones dedicated to the victims of the Sepoy Uprising. We were impressed by the reverence given to officers and civilians who had died in the Mutiny.

There was a strict policy of no photography within the building, but I approached one of the custodians and he kindly made an exception. 'One picture,' he said, but it turned out to be a few, so we put some money in the donation box. One amazing work of art that the custodians drew our attention to was a picture of John the Baptist composed entirely of letters and words taken from John's Gospel. The custodians were also eager to point out the photograph of Elizabeth II taken when she had visited in 1961. By the time we left, we felt we had learned a little bit more about St Paul's, as well as the history of its surroundings.

The Indian Museum

The museum was a walk of about a kilometer along a very busy sidewalk. Each side of the walkway were booths for cooking and selling street food, so it felt like we were walking through a kitchen/restaurant with all its smells and clatter and conversation. It also made us feel hungry, with all the lovely aromas in the air! The sidewalk was so busy, it was impossible to walk in a straight line, and the footing was also precarious because the paving stones seem to be rising in rebellion. And the noise was incredible, augmented by the unceasing music of car/bus/motorbike horns in the never-ending stream of traffic. An interesting introduction to life in the big city in India. Just, walking along the sidewalk we were brought face to face with the incredible poverty and disease of the population. We saw many beggars, some with terrible disfigurements, in contrast to so many other people dressed in fine suits or beautiful saris just going about their business. A city of great contrasts.

We passed the head office of the Indian Railways, the greatest employer of personnel on the planet. This statistic is hard to comprehend until you realize that every single level crossing in the country employs several staff to raise and lower the barriers—which we had observed in Bangalore—and then there is a multitude of drivers, station personnel, ticket clerks and administrators. It all adds up to a massive corporation.

The Indian Museum is in a classical building that was once white but is now a rather grubby grey. Like many of the buildings we visited, we entered from the street through a security screening; bags are checked individually and then scanned by a metal detector. They are very security conscious!

The building inside and out is in a state of genteel decay. It is a thoroughly old-fashioned museum, as we discovered when we entered the first gallery containing fossil bones. It was a time capsule of museum practice of a century ago; long glass and wooden display cases filled with varnished specimens, all carrying labels with their Latin names. It was all glass, bones dust and mahogany. As an exhibition of ancient museum practice, it was wonderful—you could still sense those academics of past ages cataloging away—but an appealing display it was not. It was a display to teach and study, not a display to entertain or inform.

The display of ancient stone carvings from pre-British Empire era archaeological sites was incredible. Two sites had been excavated in the 19th century and the remains transported to the museum. The quality and extent of the carving was extraordinary; it was difficult to understand how such detail could have been carved so finely 2,500 years ago. One thing that impressed us was the similarity with sculptures we had seen in the British Museum exhibition on Troy. One of the exhibits there was a depiction of the Trojan Horse from Northern India, and here we were looking at more sculptures of that genre. In some of these carvings the Buddha was represented in a very ancient-Greek manner, so it was clear that artistic ideas had flowed from Europe to Asia, and back the other way. We couldn't get enough of this gallery.

The gallery on the history of the earth was a great surprise. Here the museum was much more up-to-date, following the more 'modern' ideas of exhibition design. There were several beautifully made charts and models that gave visitors a really good idea of the spans of time and the evolution of species. These displays appeared to be recent additions, as their colours were still bright. They made a welcome change from the dour fossils and bones. The gallery on human evolution was very well laid out, although the models of the  early hominid species were quite out of date; Neanderthal man was exactly the way the Victorians imagined him. Interestingly, the label stated that no

Neanderthal genes existed in the modern human population, which we now know is not true. Need for an update there.

At this point fatigue—museum and otherwise—had set in, so we decided to flag down a classic yellow cab. The driver didn't know where we wanted to go, but a gentleman on the street helped us explain the address with the help of our tourist map. Then the driver declared that it would be 500 rupees. Bob opened the door and began to climb out, whereupon the driver shouted '300!' Bob replied with '200!' and the deal was done. This was 40 rupees more than the morning journey, but not a bad compromise. We quickly learned it was a good idea to bargain before getting into a taxi, and it was a good idea to be realistic with the offer or the taxi would drive away. The drive back was accompanied by the usual roar of traffic and the din of horns, and it was made a little less comfortable by the ancient suspension of the cab.

We were in for a lovely surprise when we went up to our hotel room. Housekeeping had been through and had produced a 'sculpture' on the bed of a pair of lovely swans, made from towels. There were red petals and leaves scattered all round and it was quite beautiful. We were touched by this lovely motif, and it was a beautiful end to a very interesting day of exploring. Almost a shame to take it apart and use the towels.

Eden Garden and the Maidan

The following morning, we decided to make our way to Eden Garden. Our ever-helpful staff called for an Uber taxi, which took us along the bank of the Hooghly River and dropped us off outside the cricket stadium, as important a facility to India as a hockey arena is in Canada. A short walk brought us to the gates of Eden Garden, a beautifully kept space with neat lawns and flower beds, an old-fashioned bandstand, avenues of royal palms, and some really amusing sculptures made of flowers. They are set up to show off the plants: a peacock with a tail made out of multicoloured flowers all spreading out; an upturned barrel pouring out a flow of flowers; and several floral sculptures of people. We found an irregular pond with small bridges over its inlets, a Japanese garden, and an extensive herbal nursery.

It was wonderful to see what could be done with floral arrangements

It was restful to just walk around the park and enjoy the relative quiet and clean air, while enjoying all it had to offer. After this delight-ful visit, we crossed the road and walked beside the eastern edge of the Maidan, where horses were grazing. Whose they were we had no idea, but they were clearly in good condition. We paused and admired the massive Eden Gardens cricket stadium—the 'Lords of Asia'—where so much great cricket has been played. Wandering along we came to a large cenotaph-like structure, which we learned was a memorial to soldiers lost in the First World War. It was a most moving monument.

While pausing at a bench under a tree to enjoy the lunch we'd brought with us, two guys came by and insisted on being photographed with us. Then one of them called his wife—or perhaps girlfriend—and we had a nice video chat with her too. Our lunch was a bit delayed, because of that enjoyable interaction. Sometimes I wonder how far round the world my picture has

been sent. Already we have been photographed frequently during this trip and, growing up in Trinidad, I was recorded numerous times. I am flattered that people still want to take a picture of a couple of rather out-of-shape older people. There's no accounting for it.

In the near distance we had spotted an intriguing tall white column. We had to investigate, which included crossing the road again (we were getting to be experts in this area) and headed for it. We passed through a park gate, walked along an avenue, and found we were beside a cricket ground with a game in progress. Of course, we had to stop and watch a couple of overs before continuing our stroll.

Indians are great cricket fans, and it was good to see some of their players in action. We finally arrived at the column we had seen from far away. It was initially dedicated to Sir James Outram, a 19th century governor, but later dedicated to Indians who had fallen in battle.

Horses roaming on the maidan. Whose they were was anyone's guess, but somebody knew

By now we were ready to go back to the hotel, so it was time for the taxi ritual. After watching many taxis pass us by, while waving industriously, one stopped. The regular taxis have 'No Refusal' written on the side. However, when we told the driver where we wanted to go, he refused. There was no use arguing as Bob found out when the driver decided to pull away while he still had his head stuck in the window. In the end, a white taxi showed up and a deal was made for about twice what Uber had charged on the way in. The driver also took us on a very scenic route, which included a loop around Science City, but as we were on a fixed fare it didn't matter. Back in our room we found white swans on the bed this time, surrounded by a profusion of seductive flowers. A beautiful welcome after a long day of exploring.

Dinner had its highlights. We sat down to dine, and a young waiter came up and told us of a cocktail he had invented, and would we like to try one at no charge? But of course! It was a quite thick orange coloured concoction that tasted quite pleasant. I detected lime in it and thought perhaps the alcohol was gin. We were halfway through it when he came back, so we asked him about the constituents. I was right about the lime, but the alcohol was vodka and the colouring was turmeric, which he had ground and prepared himself. He was very happy with our approval. Then, when dinner came, the lady from the restaurant desk came by to chat, and we heard a great deal about her family life. It is so nice when people come over and just chat. We enjoy listening to their stories and, it seems, they enjoy us listening to them. Following dinner, we retired for the night, once again regretfully destroying the swans.

SCIENCE CITY

Our explorations the following morning took us to Science City, about a kilometer from our hotel. Since it was so close, we decided to walk. We confirmed the opening hours with the hotel concierge, but when telling them we were going to walk, there was a great raising of eyebrows. As we started our walk, we realized it would take us alongside a very busy road, and we would need to cross a very wide and busy intersection. As we plotted our route, we began to understand the surprise of the staff. It actually wasn't too bad as we were walking on a separate path beside the road, but the din of traffic was appalling.

Science City occupies quite a few acres with its gardens and modernistic buildings. There are domes, half-domes and spirals, and it all looked very futuristic. On entering the area, you find a neatly laid-out garden with trimmed hedges and flowerbeds, with whirling water-driven sculptures in pools and a quite large maze made out of waist-high hedges. A gondola ride of about half a kilometer long and 20 meters high goes right over the whole park. Once inside the entrance there was a choice of several buildings, each with its own theme. Unfortunately, the earth sciences building wasn't open, which was a pity because once your visit is finished you emerge through the giant mouth of a fiberglass dinosaur. We were imagining the comments from friends and relatives, when we said we had walked through the mouth of an extinct beast! It was not to be.

Science City and the gondola

As in the Museum of India, we learned there was a large section in this hall devoted to human evolution. This really made us appreciate the contrast between the culture of India, which emphasizes education through science, and the contrast with the culturally backward parts of the USA where 'creation museums' and legislation against teaching are used to keep people in a state of ignorance.

In our visit to the Space and Technology Building we were very pleasantly surprised because the main floor was dominated by a wide range of physics demonstrations, laying out acoustics, levers, aviation, optics, magnetism, and so on. It was akin to the Museum of Science and Technology in Ottawa, only much more complete. In addition to the demonstrations, one wall was covered with ball machines, where steel balls traveled through tracks. And there were compressed air tubes where balls could be sent from one location to another. The designers seemed to have achieved the ideal combination of

play and learning. Some of the machines were not working, but the same could be said of the displays in Ottawa on any given day.

Along one wall of the lower floor there was a huge revelation: a very detailed display of the novel Corona virus outbreak, dealing with its history, the geography of its spread, and even its biochemistry. There were three large panels with very professional graphics and tons of information. All of this had been put together in the space of a month, and it was regularly updated.

Two museum employees in blue uniform were standing by the display, so we congratulated them on a great job. They were very pleased. They told us that the museum authorities considered it important for the general public to learn as much as they could about this issue. It would be nice if our museums could create exhibits as quickly about timely issues. This was the first time we had heard the title 'COVID-19.' This was just the beginning of the pandemic and all that it entailed.

The upper part of the building was laid out in a descending spiral, so visitors took an elevator to the top floor and worked their way down. Here there were wonderfully clear graphics of animal and plant cell formation, with much more detailed information than we are used to. The best part of this display was the exhibit labeled Power of 10. It started with a close-up graphic of a girl on a swing in the Science Park, viewed from above. The next panel was a power of 10 greater, so you saw the girl on the swing and the surrounding playground. Next was a view of the district of Kolkata with the entire Science Park at its centre. At this point the girl was invisible. This progression continued through to the continent of India, the entire world, the solar system, and so on out among the galaxies. Then the big surprise: back to the girl on the swing, but this time going a power of 10 smaller: a patch of skin on the cheek, the micro-structure of the skin, the protein molecules, the atoms, until you entered the subatomic world of electrons and quarks. This was perhaps the best demonstration of scale we have ever seen.

We continued down the sloping spiral to a long row of fish tanks containing quite a variety of species including sharks and piranhas, and some of the more common tropical aquarium fish, like tetras and koi. The end of the ramp led out of the building, and by this time we were ready to head for the exit. Now for the gondola ride! You had to buy a ticket for the ride and we were warned that it took you out of the ticketed area of the park; you would have to buy another ticket if you wanted to get back in. The ride was really great as it took us over the park at a height, so we could get a good overall view.

We got off the ride (Bob wished it had been longer and hoped we could go round again) found the cafeteria and had tea. The girl behind the counter gave us small cups of very milky spiced tea, and then asked if she could take a selfie with us. Of course, she could. Bob paid for the tea and she asked for a tip, which was the first time anyone had actually asked. It was fine; she was young and charming, and the small tip pleased her.

Then it was back on the road to negotiate our walk back to the hotel. We arrived without any problems and the guard at the front door asked us how we had enjoyed Science City. It was lovely to see how interested the staff were in our activities. They were always pleased with our positive comments and agreed with some of our less than positive reaction to some things.

This time, when we got back to our room there were no swans, but rather a big lotus flower made of white, pink, and green towels and, wonderfully, a footbath with hand-written instructions from Shubhendu, the housekeeper.

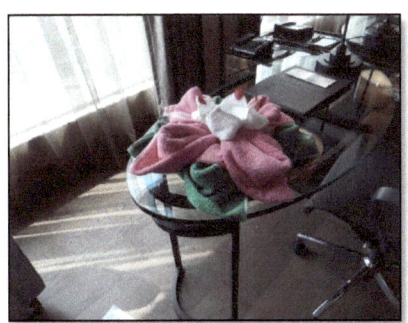

There was a package of Epsom salts and a loofah, so we both did as we were told, and our feet felt the better for it. A lovely and relaxing end to our very interesting day.

Ganges River Cruise

On our last day in India, we booked a river cruise along the Ganges for the afternoon, into the early evening. We would be flying to Thailand at the horrible time of 1:40 a.m. the following day. We packed our suitcases and left a nice tip and a 'thank you' note for our creator of swans, lotuses and footbaths and went down to breakfast. Since we were not sure about the timing of lunch, we made sure to have a really good breakfast. As we were sitting there going through our upcoming plans, our server and the lady from the desk brought us some presents. The first of them was a slice of very rich chocolate cheesecake, adorned with berries and with 'bon voyage' written on the plate in chocolate sauce. What could we do? Of course, we had to eat it! This was followed by two small cardboard boxes nicely tied up with ribbons, containing more goodies for the journey. Then there was the—by now—obligatory photo session. We left an envelope at their desk with a nice tip. We had been so spoilt by the staff at this hotel, we were sorry to leave them. The high standard that was set here would be hard to beat.

We placed our luggage in the care of the concierge and then had them whistle-up an Uber to take us into town, close to Millennium Park where our boat tour started. The park is divided in two, with the piers and docks for the tour boats in the middle. Once we'd bought our tickets—which was the usual bureaucratic rigmarole—we had a little time to spare. We bought tickets to the park and enjoyed our first view of the Hooghly, which is what the Ganges is called at this point. One thing we couldn't help but notice was the absolute sea of garbage on the shores of the river, with lots more floating in it.

Our tour boat boasted a crazy Egyptian theme with a huge golden figurehead of a peacock at the bow, and a pointed tail at the rear. Inside the theme was also Egyptian, with every surface carved or painted with sculptures and decorations. We climbed to the upper deck with about 20 others and watched while the boat pulled away from the shore and headed upstream. Our tour guide gave a running commentary of the features we were passing, but like many tour guides through a loud speaker, it was mostly incomprehensible to us. There were many ghats on the banks of the river, essentially sets of wide steps leading down to the water. These are used for all sorts of recreational and religious purposes; we passed bathing ghats with their associated temples, where people perform their ritual bathing, and a 'burning ghat' with attached crematorium where ashes were scattered. Historic buildings from the days of the Raj were also pointed out. We passed under a massive cantilever bridge with the traffic high above us hooting and rumbling.

The turning point of the tour was a beautiful temple in a park at the water's edge. Bob disembarked while I stayed in the lounge and started talking with a lady who had also stayed on the boat. She thought she would be slow and would hold back her friends, and I told her that was why I had stayed on board. We had a lovely conversation over a wide range of topics. She had visited family in Canada and enjoyed it, although at one point she was being driven on a highway and she didn't like it at all. There were no street lights and the 'jungle' was on both sides of the road! I enjoyed that interpretation of what was likely the Trans-Canada Highway. Our chat was a lot of fun and at the end of it she volunteered to share a taxi with us, as she lived near our hotel.

The boat was due to be back at Millennium Park by 7:00 but it was clear that the timing was 'flexible.' From his vantage point on shore, Bob watched three ferries dock, fill up and depart for the other side of the river before it was our turn. At one point I could see him on the pier waving to me. He got pictures of the boat, but at this point the lighting was not good. By now, the sun had set so we passed the lights of Kolkata on our return trip. The return was surprisingly quick as we were now headed downstream. As we passed under one major bridge it was all lit up in changing colours.

Once we were off the boat, this charming lady tried to call an Uber with no success, so we walked over to a rank of the yellow Ambassador cabs and let her do the wheeling and dealing, although there was not much of that. It was mainly outright refusals from cabs which had 'no refusal' printed on the doors! Thank goodness we were with her, or we would likely have been waiting for a cab for a very long time. She was able to cajole and argue with the cab drivers in a way we couldn't. Finally, after 'talking' with about three cab drivers, or maybe more, a reluctant driver agreed to take us for 400 rupees, about three times the actual cost. We were all tired, we all wanted to get home, so we climbed in. We chatted on the way home, which made the drive much more enjoyable, and this time Bob was able be part of it, rather than languishing on the dock, waiting to climb on board. While we could see the Marriott close by, the taxi driver took a wrong turning and we watched it disappearing behind us. We had him make a U-turn and we eventually got there. We said goodbye to the nice lady—sadly we never did get her name—and thankfully entered the hotel and got our luggage. Another surprise: the concierge staff also wanted pictures, so we all posed before the cab came. They also got a 'thank you' note and a reward.

The ride to the airport, clearing security, checking in our luggage was the usual boring task, made worse by our dragged-out fatigue. Finally, a short rest in the priority lounge, and we were able to board, thankful for the seat upgrade with increased legroom we had received on check-in. We were finally on our way to meet our friends in Bangkok.

Chapter Seven: Thailand

We would be staying a few days in Bangkok, then flying to Chiang Mai where we would meet our friends Zac and Anna, who live in Hong Kong. On the overnight flight to Bangkok, we had been upgraded to bulkhead seats, so it was a bit more comfortable. I was able to sleep a little, but Bob wasn't so lucky: behind him was the most colossal bore he had ever witnessed, who talked non-stop for the entire flight to a young lady who had the misfortune to be seated beside him. He had all sorts of gratuitous advice on avoiding sexual violence, all of which Bob found rather creepy. Thankfully, I missed most of this while sleeping.

Bangkok

On arrival we found that the Coronavirus was being taken seriously, and that temperature checks at the arrivals gate were necessary. In retrospect this was ominous, but it didn't really seem to bother us at the time. The airport is a long way out of the centre, and the Marriott hotel shuttle car went quite quickly and smoothly at first, but soon the trip became slower and slower. We felt shades of Kolkata as we sat motionless in one traffic jam after another. We eventually arrived, checked in, and fell into bed for a good long snooze, waking at about 11:30, perhaps a little refreshed.

We planned our exploration of Bangkok with visits to Wat Phra Kaew (the site of the Emerald Buddha), Wat Phta Chetuphon, which houses the Reclining Buddha, and the Grand Palace. The front desk staff called a tuk-tuk for us. Unlike the tuk-tuks in Kolkata, they have souped up motorcycle engines and go very fast. The tuk-tuk took us to the nearest Sky Train station where we found our way around, bought the necessary tickets, and negotiated the change of train from Sky Train to metro. The escalator out of the metro station brought us up right in front of the lovely Museum Siam. After a quick look inside the door, we made plans to come back later.

Wat Phra Kaew

The Wat Phra Kaew, just a short walk away, had been recommended to us. This temple complex is over-the-top decorated in mirrors and gold, and every other colour of the rainbow. It was stunning to see so many statues of the Buddha. The temple was dedicated to the Emerald Buddha, which stands about 66 centimetres high and is carved from a single jade stone. It is said this statue will bring prosperity and pre-eminence to every country where it resides. On entering the building, we found many people sitting on the floor and meditating. It was a quiet and peaceful place, and as tourists we felt we

were intruding on their meditations. In an adjacent temple building there was a wonderful central hall with a golden seated Buddha, while around the room there were cupboards with a large number of holy vessels. In the courtyard there were many beautiful salas housing artifacts from other countries, Cambodia and Java being two we noticed. We enjoyed admiring these creations while wondering what they represented. There were so many lovely buildings to see and admire we could only go through a few of them. Every-thing in this precinct was gorgeously decorated in gold and paint and mirrors. It reminded me of some of the highly decorated cathedrals of Europe, and I wondered what the Buddha and Jesus Christ would have thought of this ostentatious show of wealth, so opposed to their teachings.

WAT PHTA CHETUPHON

After enjoying Wat Phra Kaew, we took a short walk to Wat Phta Chetuphon where the Reclining Buddha lies. This is a huge statue, forty-six metres long and three metres high. It was built with a brick core, modelled and shaped with plaster, and then finally gilded. Seeing the Reclining Buddha was a weird experience. It was so big that I couldn't relate to it; there was no perspective where you could view the whole thing. The crowds in the room were talking, shuffling around and taking pictures, while some people were placing offerings in the designated bowls. I am aware that for many devout Buddhists, this is a site of pilgrimage and a place to honour the Buddha, but it didn't feel that way to me. It was too noisy and chaotic. I found the Emerald Buddha to be in a much calmer space, and it felt more 'holy' in consequence.

(Left) The Reclining Buddha's gigantic feet

THE MUSEUM SIAM

The theme of the museum is 'decoding Thainess' and there are two floors devoted to this. The question being posed was 'What is it to be Thai?' and the answer was hopefully provided in the displays. The approach resonated 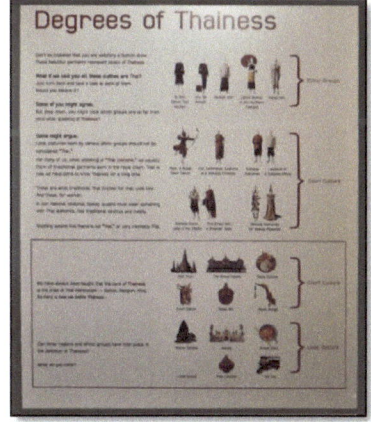 with us because we often see the same question asked in Canada. It seems that both cultures tend to define themselves by 'what we are not, rather than, what we are' so finding this common thread in the Museum Siam was familiar. The displays ranged from 'traditional' Thai artifacts to others brought from other cultures, which all added to the question. One display featured a checklist of objects and practices, some of which were Thai and others that had been imported from other cultures. Thainess was expressed in categories of Ethnic Groups, Court Culture and Local Culture, but we felt that the displays asked more questions than they answered. It was very interesting to observe these comments, and relate these to our own experiences with identity in Canada.

One spectacular display was a giant table about three meters wide by six meters long in a darkened room. An audio commentary began describing the history of Thailand while illuminated display cases containing artifacts and models rose out of the surface. As the show progressed more and more of these vitrines rose and sank, until at the end the whole lot emerged to the sound of the national anthem. It was extremely well done and, of course, Bob tried to peer through a gap in the side of the table to check out the mechanism.

Still, after all we had seen and read in the museum, I am not really sure what Thainess really is. I feel with all the influences coming into any country, it is hard to define what is inherent and what are outside influences, which are then assimilated into the culture. It might be a losing proposition, and globalization will only make it less easy to define.

We did have a salutary experience on the metro; due to the pollution in Bangkok, I was coughing a bit, but nothing too serious. However, a lady sitting a couple of seats away immediately got up and moved to the other end of the car. Fortunately, there was lots of room so she found a seat far from this potential source of disease. This was in the very early days of COVID-19; very few people were wearing masks, but she clearly wasn't about to take a chance.

Having arrived at a metro station a few minutes away from our hotel, Bob thought it would be quick and easy to take a tuk-tuk, so we went to the rank where they were parked, showed the driver the map, and off we went. It wasn't long before Bob said that he was sure we should have arrived by now, and our anxiety only increased as the journey continued in dense traffic with lots of stops and starts. Being in an open vehicle so close to herds of stalled motorbikes and cars, we were getting very polluted. Eventually we pulled up at the Marriott. Not our one; another one, many kilometers away.

Clearly, the driver hadn't looked at the map he was shown. He went in and got directions from the doorman and off we went again. By this time, we were both feeling poisoned and the drive only got worse and worse. We pulled up at another Marriott—still not ours—and we were on the verge of abandoning this guy and calling a cab. He got directions from another doorman and off we went yet again. Finally, feeling sick and dizzy, we were deposited at our hotel, well over half an hour later, for a drive of maybe 10 minutes. But we did get to see a lot of downtown Bangkok through the haze of pollution. Just a note, Kolkata was never this bad!

I staggered out of the tuk-tuk and sat on the sofa in the hotel foyer, feeling an asthma attack coming on and just trying to breathe. The porters at the concierge desk were standing and chatting with each other, and didn't even look over, let alone ask me how I was doing. One part of me was glad, but the other part said, 'One of your guests is not looking well, and you can't be bothered to ask if they need help!' This was such a contrast to the solicitous treatment had we received in Kolkata that I was a bit shocked. Perhaps this was just the attitude of two individual, and not the policy of the hotel, but it did leave a bad impression. The asthma issue persisted throughout our stay in Bangkok.

Wat Benchamabophit

Our tuk-tuk experience of the day before was still raw in our memories (and lungs) so this time we took a taxi. The taxi driver knew the way, but he did keep leaning over and showing laminated brochures of markets, theatres and restaurants while making pointed suggestions. No thank you: we are going to Wat Benchamabophit, the Marble Temple.

This is a lovely building with a long history. Parts of it were clad in marble about a century ago, but it still has many features of its earlier state.

The first thing that impressed us was the scale: this is a small building set in a wide precinct, so it has none of the overpowering quality of Wat Phra Kaew. As usual, before entering the temple precinct we removed our shoes, and went into the courtyard. The external decorations were as beautiful as others we'd seen, but this was the first time we'd encountered lots or marble being used. The colours and patterns were quite gorgeous, but the nice thing was that the ceiling beams and rafters were all in their original decoration. We also found – although it might be imagination – that there was more sense of reverence here than in the larger venues. It was certainly quieter as there were fewer visitors.

We had noticed many billboards, posters and notices requesting respect for the Buddha: Don't use his image on T-shirts, don't make tattoos of him, speak quietly in the temples, etc. It is clear that reverence for the Buddha is very deeply rooted in Thai culture, and these injunctions are reactions to an increasing secularism. Certainly, the hubbub of the large tourist sites drives away any feeling of awe. This little temple redressed the balance.

Outside, and with shoes back on, we visited the gardens. There was a small canal crossed by a sharply hump-backed bridge, where fountains were playing. It was a very restful scene, especially as the sun was now high and it was getting very hot. As we explored further, we found a house with a lovely

veranda, on which were several ceremonial drums. Some were carved from huge pieces of wood, but the largest horizontal one was made from a whole hollow tree trunk. It would have been nice to hear them played, but they didn't seem to be used. We just had to imagine to incredible sound they would have created.

ANANTASAMAKHOM PALACE

After we left the temple precinct, we crossed the road and made our way to where we thought the Anantasamakhom Palace might be. A long, hot walk along a busy and noisy street brought us to a wide boulevard with the palace at its end. It's a white, ornate building in an Italianate style, erected at the beginning of the 20th century. Along one side of the boulevard was a large space guarded by sentries, and this turned out to be the Royal Palace Grounds, to which we would not be admitted. To one side of the white palace was a beautiful little temple, which we thought was probably part of the palace precinct, but could not find any information about it.

By now we were very hot and tired, so we decided to hail a cab. Now came the challenge: trying to explain where we wanted to go was not easy. We had the map out and pointed to our hotel, and after a little while, the driver agreed that the mission was possible. All went well until Bob noticed that we had passed our turning and were continuing blithely in the opposite direction. We soon pulled up at a Marriott: one of the other ones! It was the second one we had visited on our ill-fated tuk-tuk ride! We slapped down the fare, climbed out and crossed the street to ask the Marriott staff for directions. Thankfully, our Marriott was within walking distance of this one —they gave us very good directions—but it was a long, hot trek before we made it back. We really felt we were not having much success with the local transportation system!

After a long rest, and a room-service lunch, Bob went out to take pictures of the small shrine not far from us, where dedication ceremonies were underway almost all day. People were buying garlands of beautiful yellow flowers and covering the shrine with them, while in a roofed-over space, dancers, singers and a small orchestra played. This scene provided a sharp contrast to the roaring traffic and the vast concrete arches of the Sky Train just paces away.

Chiang Mai

We flew to Chiang Mai the next day and our friends, Zac and Anna, were there to meet us at the airport. They had flown in about two hours before from Hong Kong, but knew Chiang Mai very well from previous business and pleasure trips. We all got into the Shangri-La Hotel limousine—very nice indeed—and off we went, chatting all the while as we caught up with things. The hotel is over-the-top luxurious, and while the staff were taking our luggage and checking us in, they sat us down in the lounge for a complementary glass of wine.

The first thing to do, before tourism could start, was to check into my continuing asthma issues, so the hotel staff nurse was summoned for a visit. She couldn't prescribe the steroid inhaler I needed, but she arranged for us to go by ambulance to a nearby hospital, where I was checked out and given a prescription at the hospital's pharmacy. This was all part of the hotel service and our only cost was the inhaler I was prescribed to treat my lungs! They even took us back to the hotel in the ambulance, and the doctor came along too, as he and Zac had been discussing the Corona Virus outbreak. Although the hotel practiced screening and temperature checks at the door, and masking was recommended, we had no idea how serious things would become over the next few months.

I spent the second day in Chiang Mai with my friend Anna, spending the morning spoiling ourselves with a luxurious pedicure. Anna chose a lovely soft pink for her toenails, while I went with the golden theme of our Thailand adventures. Totally silly, but lots of fun! After our toes were done, we were taken to another room and given tea and tasty rice cookies. The tables in the spa were old fashioned treadle Singer sewing machines with the machine part taken off and replaced by a table. It took me back to my school days, when we used these machines in our sewing classes!

Meanwhile Bob spent the morning with our friend Zac, checking out the old quarter of Chiang Mai, which is a square area enclosed by a moat. While looking at temples they also enjoyed the local coconut water and iced coffee. Of the three major temples they visited, they chose two

for the four of us to see the following day. And maybe, just maybe, a third if we had the energy left.

Zac located a drugstore and bought their entire stock of face masks and hand sanitizer to take back home to Hong Kong for his staff, as these preventive measures were totally out of stock there. News of the Coronavirus was becoming a lot more concerning, and it seemed appropriate to prepare for it, so we all chose to wear masks in crowded indoor spaces. I was happy to wear one as it reduced the amount of pollution I was exposed to.

While the four of us were enjoying spa treatment and temple spotting, our laundry—that never ending task—was being taken care of by the hotel and returned to us that afternoon. All the shirts and pants were hung up on hangers and the underwear and socks were in a wicker basket, wrapped it tissue paper and with a lavender sachet included. Most luxurious! Very different from laundry day at home.

Wat Chedi Luang

The next day saw us checking out the various sites the guys had scoped out. We took a taxi to the first one, Wat Chedi Luang, and made our way through the temple complex. The buildings were all wonderful, with lots of gold, flowers and decorations, and quite impressive to see. The first temple we entered was very peaceful, with a number of worshippers kneeling in front of the Buddha. It was a place to be quiet and reflective. Another contrast with the larger sites in Bangkok.

The largest feature of this temple complex was the Wat Chedi Luang itself, which was originally built in the late 14th century. At that time the Chedi was 60m square with a height of 80m and was the home of the Emerald Buddha, Thailand's most sacred religious relic. In 1545, as a result of an earthquake, a part of the Chedi fell and it was reduced to half its height. The top of the Chedi was never restored, but its height is still very impressive. Restoration work was completed in 1992, when the naga (water serpent) staircase and the statues of elephants on each of the building's faces were replaced. After walking right around this enormous structure, it was time for a pause for refreshment in a little café in the temple precinct.

WAT PHRA SINGH

It is said that, 'If you can only see one temple in Chiang Mai, the Gold Pagoda is the one to see.' The Gold Pagoda, Wat Phra Singh, fulfilled its billing. We encountered another reclining Buddha, not as large as the one in Bangkok, but impressive nevertheless. We were interested to see that there were fewer tourists and the majority of those visiting these temples were devotees of the Buddha. Unlike the crowded sites in Bangkok, we found the tourists more respectful of the sites and of the worshippers. Again, we came across notices admonishing people to be respectful of the Buddha's image. Sometimes I think the Christian churches should have notices like this.

The wonderful golden stupa of Wat Phra Singh is an amazing sight; a huge structure entirely covered in gold. It was examined closely by Bob because he was interested in finding how it was made. On the corners where the coating had been worn smooth you could discern the various layers. The brick core had been clad with sheet metal soldered at the edges, then coated with a yellow underlayer on which gold leaf was laid. Gold-leafing an entire structure this size would be a huge and costly undertaking.

Two days was too short a time to see much of Chiang Mai, but now it was time to do some more exploring. The next day we were going to drive north to Chiang Rai, which borders Myanmar to the north west and Laos to the east.

CHIANG RAI

We left Chiang Mai in a rather lovely large van, very fancy inside and highly decorated with fancy moldings and trim. It took a good while to drive out of Chiang Mai, which we learned was quite extensive, before getting to the highway that would take us north. We passed though a number of villages, which resembled tropical villages almost anywhere in the world. However, the store names were in both English (most of the time) and Thai. Apart from this, they all resembled the villages we had seen in India, or even Trinidad! It seems that villages and towns throughout the world create similar patterns because that is how they work best.

While we were visiting Thailand in February, we noticed that the ground was pretty dry, and the fields were somewhat brown and uncultivated. We learned that the rains were not due until April, but the rice paddies were being tended and were well irrigated. As we drove past, we noticed some of the paddies were very wet and newly sown, while in others the rice had grown above water level and was filling the area.

Eventually, we left the flatter agricultural land and started climbing into the mountains, and here we were reminded very strongly of many of our travels up north in Canada: the dreaded word 'construction.' The highway was being widened, and it appeared that the whole road was being done all at once! This meant construction zones were on and off for miles, with long stretches of driving along unpaved surface while the work was being done.

Then, thankfully, the road would clear: 'Ah, it's finished' you would say. But, no. All to soon, we meet the next phase of construction. Finally, back to highway driving, and a sigh of relief… Wait, there's more! Here come the big trucks again! And so, it went for a very long time. We did eventually come to what looked like a finished road although construction did rear its busy head just once more. Eventually we did drive out of it, but it took a lot of time and made our trip longer than it should have been.

We stopped for a short break in a market area, no doubt set up for travellers to pause and stretch. There were many stalls selling food and drinks for hungry people, and the usual tourist trinkets and clothes. I bought a lovely patterned skirt from one of these for the outrageous sum of $4.00! Now I just needed a top to go with it.

The best part of this rest stop was the natural hot springs shooting and bubbling up to about waist height into basins made of bricks! There were three of them, two on the side we parked on and one on the seething, frothing water for a while and then noticed a man waving a small basket on a stick in the hot water. He was boiling eggs and selling them! We didn't buy one, but thought it was an enterprising use of these thermal springs. I was sure somewhere in the locale there must have been a spa or pool set up for visitors to enjoy.

Just before arriving in Chiang Rai, we stopped at a strange farm theme park, which included a zoo, rides in trolleys, and other fun activities. It was a rather strange place, and so close to our destination that we suspected our driver got some sort of premium for stopping there. We did buy a bottle of Thai wine! We had no idea what it would be like, but thought it would be interesting to try.

Finally, we arrived at Chiang Rai and found the guest house where we were staying. The house belonged to a friend of Zac's who rented it to us at a very cheap rate. It was bare-bones, but at the same time quite charming. We settled in, and found that our room had the four-poster bed! No curtains I am afraid. That evening we went out for a late lunch/early supper at a very nice restaurant that Anna had found. It was in a delightful spot on the river and the food was delicious.

The Blue Temple
After supper we walked to the Blue Temple, which is a new one, founded in

2005 and completed in 2016/17. Everything in this complex was painted blue with weird and fantastic overdone sculptures (left: a gate guardian) lit with UV light, and dominated by a giant white fibreglass Buddha. We looked around and took the requisite pictures to say we had been there, but really… It had none of the reverence we had felt in other temples, and we didn't see any monks, or other devotees, or even local people except those in the booths selling trinkets! It certainly was different from any temple we had seen before, but we were not sure how we felt about it as a religious building. There was not a trace of reverence.

Later, Bob and Zac went grocery shopping, while Anna and I went back to the house to chill out for a while. It was starting to get dark, and it appeared that none of the lights in the house were working! After a groping search of what seemed like ages, we found the switch, and the lights came on. We were both very relived, and glad we could finally see where we were going and what we were doing. When the guys came back with the groceries, we relaxed with a glass of wine on the veranda and planned our adventures for the next day.

THE WHITE TEMPLE

The next visit was quite remarkable. We had breakfast in the same restaurant as the night before, and this time we were led to an upper terrace overlooking the river and a large stand of bamboo. It was a long, lingering meal and quite delicious, after which we headed off to the White Temple courtesy of a grab taxi. This was quite a long ride out of town, but when we got there, we found a huge precinct of tourist shops, cafes, etc., all clustered round the most bizarre building

I think I have ever seen. This was a Buddhist temple that had gone to ruin and had been bought back and rehabilitated by Thai artist Chalermchai Kositpipat, and he had really let his imagination run wild. Every surface of the central temple was decorated with flame motifs, and all painted white with attached mirrors. The temple was approached by a bridge across a small moat. On each side of the walkway were hundreds of life-sized hands sticking up out of the ground in all sorts of poses. Some held skull caps, into which people could throw coins. The temple was painted inside with scenes from the life of Buddha, but also had depictions of the modern world like the Twin Towers, spaceships, and cultural icons like Batman and Elvis. They were all meticulously painted in great detail; Kositpipat is a great artist. Even with all this artistic flamboyance, this is still a 'working' temple and a place of prayer, so you take off your shoes and no photography is allowed inside. In front of the figure of Buddha there was a square red carpet reserved for those who wished to pray, and even in a space dominated by tourists, there was still an air of reverence.

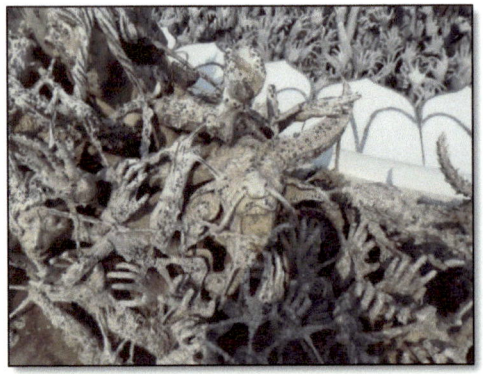

The White Temple sits in a huge complex of buildings. We walked around the whole complex marveling at the extent of the place, and the number of structures. Most were in white, like the main temple, but some others were covered in gold and equally decorated. One amazing feature was a covered walkway about 50 m long, with countless thousands of metal and bead pendants hanging from its rafters. These were sold at a stall so people could write a wish or a prayer on them and have them hung up. There is still room for more, as one section of roof is still waiting to be filled.

We crossed over a golden bridge to the art gallery and gift shop, where the artist's prints and sculptures are on sale. I really liked the T-shirts, and bought a lovely black one with gold motif, which will look well with the skirt I had bought the previous day. It had been a most interesting day, and we were all astonished by the White Temple.

We had a delicious meal in very pleasant surroundings, another charming restaurant on the river. Because we were seated outside, the waiter brought us bug spray to ward off the mosquitoes, not something we would see at home, but quite common here. After dinner it was time to get back to the house and think about returning to Chiang Mai the next day.

One our last day in Chiang Rai, after organizing our bags for travelling back to Chiang Mai, we all went out for a walk. We went one way while Zac and Anna went another, as they were seriously walking while we were merely strolling! We walked slowly through the area, just enjoying looking around. As we walked back to the house, we came upon a garden full of cages where fighting cocks were kept. We had heard them crowing at all hours of the day and part of the night, so now we finally learnt where they lived. There were at least 10 cages in this one yard and, I suspect, there were other houses with at least as many cocks!

The drive back was fine; long and tedious, but it seemed to be quicker than the drive down. Our only stop on this trip was at a police checkpoint! We finally arrived at the hotel, tired and stiff, to find a lovely surprise. Our rooms had been upgraded, and both couples now enjoyed lounging in executive suites! The suites were very large, with a living/meeting room the size of an average hotel bedroom, with its own powder room and a large office desk. The bedroom was separated by a table into two sections with the bed on one side and a divan on the other. The table had a large TV on a swivel so you could watch from the bed or the divan! The bathroom was very large, with all the usual amenities and two separate wash basins. Altogether over-the-top. Oh, to be an executive with an expense account! Still, it's nice to see how the other half lives. In fact, I think this suite was twice the size of the small apartment Bob and I rented in downtown Toronto many, many years ago!

Ping River Cruise

On our last full day in Chiang Mai, we thought it would be interesting to see the city from another point of view by taking a cruise on the Ping River. The boat dock was in the precinct of a small temple, so while we were waiting to leave, we looked around. The decoration was as beautiful and varied as the larger and more popular temples we had visited, and the gold on the pagoda was glorious. Even the devotees of these smaller temples lavish attention on their holdings. Next to the temple—between it and the river—was a burial ground with some very elaborate and decorated grave markers.

The boat accommodated perhaps 30 passengers, but there were only about 10 or 12 when we moved away from the dock. We had noticed fewer tourists here that in Bangkok and wondered if the Coronavirus outbreak had put a stop to some non-essential travel. Our host provided a commentary, but it was far from obtrusive.

We headed up the Ping River through the city and then out into more open country. The view from the river gave us an idea of how the more prosperous lived because their properties all had docks or decks, or lawns that sloped down to the water. We were able to see the high-water mark of the river in flood. It showed us where the various property owners would need to renew their lower land once the annual flood waters had passed.

We watched people fishing, swimming, and sunbathing, passing many very nice properties. At one point we passed a man up to his waist in the water, thumping long poles into the riverbed. These were supports for a long fish net that others were spreading out. In a number of places there were floating mats of lotus pads with many flowers in bloom, and we spotted quite a number of shorebirds and one kingfisher.

The leisurely progress up the river took about an hour and then we docked at our turn-around point, disembarked from the boat onto a very rickety bamboo dock, and climbed some steps to a series of huts at the top of the riverbank. Here we were led along a winding path and into a small botanical garden where we were shown a wide variety of tropical plants, some medicinal and others edible. At the end of the walk, we were directed to a table and were offered a variety of exotic juices; the four of us chose one each and compared notes. There were some very intriguing and exotic flavours. A visit to the men's washroom was a delight: one single carved log serving both ablution and waste water discharge of both kinds.

On our return to the dock, we were shown some preserved skeletons, especially one of an elephant, as well as a rack full of equally skeletal car engines. Quite why they were there we only discovered later. As always on these boat trips the return journey was much faster as we were travelling with the flow. As we docked, there were a few smaller craft alongside, and we saw how those skeletal car engines we had seen were used. An engine was attached to a swiveling steel frame, a long propeller shaft was added, and the whole assembly was used power and steer the smaller boats. Very ingenious.

Travelling over a long period of time means one's hair gets a little shaggy, so that afternoon we all went to have our hair dealt with. Again, Anna found the perfect place, a lovely little salon, and we all went to be appropriately shorn. We were warmly welcomed and discovered the owner of the establishment was married to a Canadian from Quebec who was the principal of the International School here in Chiang Mai! After a very silly and useful time we all came out looking much better.

This was our last evening in Chiang Mai before leaving for Singapore the next day, so a last celebratory and goodbye supper ended the day perfectly.

Before we left, Zac gave us several masks and bottles of hand sanitizer because of the increasing concerns about the Corona virus. On arrival at the airport, we noticed that all flights to and from China had been cancelled. Interesting. Also, a lot more people were wearing masks. Once boarded we found our flight to be scarcely half full, and while we took full advantage of this, we began to realize that the authorities were beginning to take the Corona virus seriously.

Chapter Eight: Return to Singapore

Back in Singapore, the airport was almost empty. Going through customs and immigration took very little time, and we got the impression that the staff were pleased to have somebody to process! Then it was off to the taxi line through an empty concourse. The first time we had arrived here, we were in the line-up for quite a while, but this time it was us and the attendant! We were the first passengers our taxi driver had picked up that day! We were beginning to realize the impact of the Corona virus in this part of the world.

Coming back to Singapore felt like coming back home, but with a difference. The first time we arrived, the place was going full blast; lots of tourists, a busy hotel, full restaurants, and a whole atmosphere of excitement. This time the airport was empty, the hotel was only a quarter full, and staff were being laid off. Some of the guests, who were supposed to be picking up cruises, had seen them cancelled, and were now waiting for flights to be arranged to take them home. The restaurants lining the river now had empty seats and tables. The owners and staff all worried about the future. Many people were wearing masks out-of-doors and keeping away from other people. It was a very different scene from our first visit. Fear of the Corona virus was everywhere, and the local people were taking care and hoping that it would not take hold. The newspapers were full of instructions on how to protect oneself from the virus and described the places where it originated and spread. The general feeling was of apprehension, and it could be noticed everywhere.

Singapore River Cruise

The Singapore River looks and feels like a canal with walls on each bank, and pathways and buildings running both sides of it. We thought it would be interesting to take a cruise as we'd seen tour boat docks at various points.

There was a definite lack of tourists when we boarded, and we were the only ones at our location. A little way downriver the boat called in to another dock and two other couples joined us. That was the extent of the tourists! Six people on a boat that would normally take somewhere between 20 and 30.

This was a very relaxing ride, and while we saw no fishing or other activities along the banks—the river being constrained between retaining walls—the buildings we passed showed a lot of historical interest. One large tourist area, which now has many hotels, used to be the dockland area and would have been full of ships bringing supplies to the island. As we made our way down-river, we passed a number of bronze sculptures positioned on the river walls. The most remarkable was of a group of boys playing on the wall, with on in the act of jumping off. I could just imagine all the grandchildren doing exactly this if they were allowed.

We passed under a number of bridges: the Elgin bridge had been built in the 1860s, another was one of the first suspension bridges, another the first built over the Singapore River. We passed right by the Merlion, the symbol of Singapore, and circled Marina Bay with all the highrise towers of the financial district looking down. I have no idea how many there were, but Singapore is a huge commercial and financial hub. We went up close to the Helix Bridge, which was quite different to see from the water.

We chatted with the other tourists onboard who were Australians on their way to Vietnam. We told them that our next stop was Australia, but in retrospect, I wonder if they ever made it to Vietnam, given the rate the Corona virus was spreading. After this charming river trip, we walked back from the dock to the hotel. During our regular river walks we had frequently seen the local otters, sometimes sunning themselves, other times splashing in the water. On one occasion we spotted several of them in the water playing with an empty beer can that someone had thrown away. (Floating garbage in the Singapore River is very rare, and we had watched the clean-up barge plying its way up and down several times.) We had also been told about a monitor lizard that wandered around the river, and we had tried to spot it

several times. Finally, we came across this interesting beast, and were surprised how big it actually was. We were advised not to go too close as its bite can be nasty. We were pleasantly surprised with our wildlife spotting this close to our hotel.

Raffles Hotel

We knew we would be in Singapore for our 49th Wedding Anniversary, and being so far from home we had to do something special. Naturally, given our location and its fame, Raffles Hotel was the obvious choice, and what better way than to toast our event with the traditional Singapore Sling? We also thought High Tea might be a nice treat for the occasion.

The entrance to the Raffles Hotel is spectacular and even more so when there is a Ferrari parked in front of it. We didn't have a reservation for High Tea, so while we waited for our time slot we went to the famous Long Bar for, what else, our Singapore Sling. Just as a side note, this drink was created for the ladies of a hundred years ago to appear to be a mere fruit juice, and even though it looked innocuous it was full of various forms of alcohol! We ordered one each, toasted each other, and ate lots of free peanuts from a hessian bag, dropping the shells on the floor, as is the tradition.

At the table next to us was a couple from France, and naturally we got talking… sort of. Her English was not great and his was virtually non-existent. Dad's French was okay and mine non-existent. With all of that, we managed to have a lovely time talking about a number of things, including the following coincidence. We had mentioned visiting a little church in Vic with Isabelle's family. Vic is a small town near Le Grand Besse, and amazingly a friend of theirs has a restaurant next to the church, so they knew the place well! Who would think we would meet someone in Singapore who knew of this little church in such a small town? They described the tour they were on: apparently, their tour company books the air-flights and hotels, but once in a location you can do your own thing or take the tours they offer. One of the tours, which this couple had taken, was to Easter Island to see the stone sculptures. They showed pictures and were obviously taken with them. It sounded like a good type of tour; freedom to go where you want in some places, and taking organized tours in others.

After our Singapore Slings, we went back downstairs for our High Tea date in the tearoom. This room has very clean and simple lines, all in white, and soars to three stories with a huge chandelier and balconies. We were shown to our table and our order taken. High tea for two; coffee for Bob and tea for me. It took a while for it to come, but when it did it was special. Because crab sandwiches were on the menu, they kindly made my sandwiches away from any contamination and served them on a separate

plate. The scones were served warm with clotted cream and jam. Everything else came on a silver cake stand, with different items on each of the three tiers. Everything was quite delicious and more than enough. A good way to celebrate our anniversary. One thing we did notice: nobody in this iconic place seemed worried about The Virus, but then Raffles was a wonderful place to relax and forget what was going on outside its doors.

Our final act of the day was to go down to the bar in our hotel and have a glass of red wine to celebrate this day. You may ask 'What kind of red wine?' 'Merlot we will answer.' Why merlot? Well, it was the only one they had! It was a nice end to the day, sitting on the outside deck of the bar and enjoying the warm wind coming off the river. Lovely.

Urban Redevelopment Authority Centre

Next morning, we took a 10-minute taxi ride to the Singapore City Gallery in the Urban Redevelopment Authority Centre (URA). Zac had told us about this great city planning exhibition; he was really enthusiastic, and we soon saw why. Finding the Centre in the first place was not too easy; the direction arrows took us in quite the opposite direction, and we ended up in a bare concrete stairwell! Finally, after finding someone to direct us, we made our way to the building. Not a great promotion for an Urban Planning display!

The first of the Corona precautions showed up on entering the building. 'Have you visited China?' was the first question from the lady at the door.

'Then, sign in please with full contact information.' We were told to use the hand sanitizer provided before entering. (It's strange to think that what we saw as exotic protocols soon became normal.) Once we got through all the protocols, we came to an interior garden with flowers and bushes, nice seats and even a swing chair.

Passing through this we found a huge model of the whole island, which was coupled with a video presentation on a large screen. As the various features of the island were described, they were illuminated to indicate them. Little India and Chinatown were lit in pink, the reservoirs and rivers appeared in blue, and so on. The whole presentation took about 10 minutes and detailed all aspects of Singapore's development.

Upstairs there was a display of maps showing the development of the island, from the earliest ones at the beginning of the 19th century when Stamford Raffles established his trading centre here, to the present-day modern city. About 20 display panels, with perhaps one or two maps each, showed the progressive development of Singapore. What we found most interesting was how these maps were organized: they all provided information in a structured way, and then each map pointed out three things that the viewer should know about. We read them all, and by the end of the display we felt we had a better understanding of why the people of this island accept some of the restrictions the government places on them. The maps and legends did not discuss this specifically, but it was just the overall style and content that made us think this way.

The interactive model of Singapore

The Urban Redevelopment Authority is very fond of models, and in a gallery opposite we found a wonderfully detailed one of the entire city centre, with each building lovingly built and rendered incredibly accurately. Bob had fun tracing all the places we had visited, and he was even able to locate our hotel beside the river. The buildings in some parts of the model were plain wood blocks because these represented future developments. In one small section there had even been a children's competition where very imaginative buildings had been made in white Lego. Bob was astounded at the amount of time it must have taken to build such a huge and detailed model. The URA plays a very important part in the development of this city, and no doubt those non-detailed wood blocks will become reality at some point and will be replaced with models, finely rendered in the Centre's workshops.

The modelmaking was extremely detailed and all parts beautifully finished

This display really demonstrated the emphasis on urban planning in Singapore, and also the intensity of the government desire to create a better living space for the people here. At the same time, it did not seem to allow for individuality, and while too much individuality may not be helpful, this planning process felt very contrived, reinforcing the reaction we had had to the maps. Decision-making and planning came from the top, downwards.

Along one wall of another gallery was a display of pin-and-string graphics of local animals. Drawing pins were inserted into a board, then string of various colours was wound around the pins to depict the animals. These were fun to look at, and the apparent simplicity of the medium belied the skill of the artist.

After a restorative cup of tea, we flagged down a taxi to take us back to the hotel. We got in and were rewarded by an amazing sight: the entire dashboard and the shelf below the windshield were covered with all sorts of plastic models—tanks, cars, planes, action figures, a Taj Mahal—all wired up

with coloured LEDs that flashed and winked. The rotor of a large helicopter on the passenger side spun intermittently. The helicopter was apparently linked to the car's electrical system, because it stalled at traffic lights and began to spin when the car pulled away. Between the front seats was a large yellow Ferrari, also wired with lights. This display was something you don't see every day. The driver also spent the whole ride on the phone, which was a bit confusing. At first, we didn't know if he was talking to us or somebody else! As long as he kept his eyes on the road, his conversation with whomever was fine by us.

St Andrew's Cathedral

The cathedral was built in the 1860s in the colonial neo-Gothic style, replacing an earlier church on the site. It reminded us strongly of the cathedral in Kolkata in both period and style. Unlike most churches on this pattern, the bell tower is separate from the nave. We found the west door below the tower was closed and were directed to the north transept door. There was a sign telling us that monitoring for Corona virus was in progress, but it seemed it was only done when congregations were present for services. The interior had clean lines with very little decoration, and all painted in white. The sunlight through the stained-glass windows showed beautifully on the white columns and arches.

Of most interest were the many stone and brass commemorative plaques set into the walls. Many were dedicated to those who had served in the administration of the Straits, with church missions, or in trade, and others to parents and children who had died in the colony. There were several other plaques dedicated to the victims of the 5th Native Light Infantry Mutiny of 1915, which we had not heard of before. We walked round the entire interior, examining the dedications and wondering about the people they honoured. This was a quiet and restful place.

Singapore Art Gallery

The first area we visited in the art gallery was the children's education centre. This was a wonderful space dedicated to informing children about art and helping them understand the range of possibilities. Thus, no paintings hanging on walls, but interactive spaces where they could explore and play. There were rooms set aside for crafts, containing all the tools and materials needed for making things. There were stacks of papers and coloured cardboard, pens, pencils and inks, and a variety of cutting and shaping tools. Everything needed to create works of art or craft was there. The place was very quiet, and we were among very few visitors. We talked to one of the staff who was responsible for the space and she told us that all school outings have been cancelled for health and safety reasons. This was a pity because I could imagine how it would have been with a class of kids letting their creativity go.

A large suite of rooms was devoted to *Karung Guni Boy*, a children's book character who collects stuff that people throw away and makes things of it. A *karung guni* is like a rag-and-bone man, which was a Singapore occupation years ago but is now dying out. The displays in this area included a wide range of objects made from scrap cardboard, paper, straws and other found objects, including a massive robot of packing boxes, plastic washing bowls and tableware. This whole section, together with the book, would inspire children to emulate what they saw. My overall impression of this gallery was that it combined play and creativity in a positive way, and that children would come away with a new appreciation of art and craft, and also be able to show off something they had made.

The children's book Karung Guni Boy *and a giant robot made of discarded cardboard and plastic*

We had to buy tickets for the rest of the displays. Singaporeans got in free, but visitors paid a small amount. There was a discount for senior citizens and another if you could show an airline boarding pass so, thanks to smart phones, we ended up paying very little. We took the elevator up to the first of the display galleries, which featured artworks from the 19th and 20th centuries with a particular Malay theme. There were scenes from the Straits Settlements, Malaysia, Singapore, and Bali, among others. There were some really fine paintings exhibited, but nothing that really made me stop and wonder. It's often that way in an art gallery, but every so often one work really strikes you. Not this time, however.

We went up to the roof garden where they had a dugout wooden boat on display; echoes of our West Coast art. It was beautifully decorated, and we enjoyed looking it over. Unfortunately, we couldn't find any information on it. Just before we left the gallery, we bought a copy of *Karung Guni Boy* to give to our daughter who is a teacher, to see how these ideas would work with her students.

Thinking back on this part of our trip, everywhere we visited was quiet; no tourist crowds, almost empty buildings, sparsely populated restaurants, and a sense of calm before the storm. The lack of visitors to all these tourist destinations was a sign of things to come.

We had enjoyed our time in Singapore and now we were heading to Australia to see what Down Under had to offer. We still had only a slight concern about the Corona virus, even though it was slowly pushing itself to the forefront of people's minds, because it seemed that the precautions of masking and hand washing would keep people safe.

Chapter Nine: Sydney and Alice Springs

We headed to Sydney, the third and last of our hubs, with Air Singapore. It was nice to be back in business class again. The seats were even nicer than the Swiss Air Flight. While inflight, I was reading an article in the magazine that described places to experience the Midnight Sun. There were lots of suggestions, with the huge omission of Canada and Alaska. It made the article a little incomplete! We were surprised how long the flight was—about seven hours—but fortunately we made up some time and landed in Sydney about 30 minutes early. Immigration and customs were easy, although just a bit tedious as always. My suitcase had to be x-rayed, but fortunately, the process was quick, and we were on our way to the hotel. There seemed to be very little concern about the virus; it was business as usual.

Once through all the formalities it was time to find a taxi. We had booked a Marriott hotel before we left home, but had not realized exactly where it was. Our taxi driver had difficulty finding the place, but after a long drive we found it was a long way out of town. It cost $105.00 plus taxes just to get from the airport! We realized that staying there would mean very little touristing, so we planned to find somewhere else the next day.

The next morning, we went online to one of the discount sites and found an unidentified, five-star hotel at Circular Quay for less than $150.00 a night. Only after we booked it, were we vouchsafed the name of the hotel: the Marriott! So, now we were going to be staying where we originally hoped to stay. On checking out, the hotel staff were very understanding, cancelled our reservations and wished us well for the rest of the trip.

Sydney

Once we arrived at the hotel, we settled in and then went for a walk along Circular Quay, seeing the iconic Sydney Harbour Bridge, the Opera House and, of course, Circular Quay itself. We went into the Opera House just to check it out. It is an amazing building, and we were hoping we could take in a show of some sort there, just to say we had. Then a brief walk took us up to the Botanical Gardens where we were amused to see a garden full of 'Roman ruins.' They were just a mixture of broken classical architectural elements, no doubt scavenged to make a talking point and focus. The gardens were a nice place to rest and enjoy the peace before we walked slowly back to the hotel. It was a lovely way to start our adventures in Australia.

Iconic features of Sydney that are almost too trite to print

One the way back we noticed a lovely looking creperie, The Four Frogs. We couldn't imagine where that name came from until we discovered it was run by four Bretons. After checking the menu our supper decision was made. We had Breton-style crepes, which were really delicious, and reminded us of our visit to Paris with our two grandsons several years ago. We had introduced them to Breton crepes, and they enjoyed them as much as we enjoyed these excellent ones in Sydney.

After supper we walked along the Quay and noticed bronze plaques set into the sidewalk, commemorating famous writers who had visited Australia. Joseph Conrad, Anthony Trollope, Nevil Shute, and Arthur Conan-Doyle were among them. We loved the idea of remembering these famous writers and thought how nice it would be if Ottawa did something like that for writers in Canada past and present. I am sure our writers would appreciate being honoured in this way.

Once back in our hotel room, we were relaxing and thinking about our explorations for the following day, when our door burst open! A very embarrassed man stood there; he had been given the wrong key, and thought this was his room. We reassured him we understood and were not upset, and forgot all about it. He left and went down to the desk to sort it all out, and we just laughed and went on with our planning. A little while later we received a call from the front desk apologizing for the mix up, and they were sending up some wine and tiramisu! Once it arrived, we enjoyed a small glass of wine, and stored the tiramisu in the fridge for the next day.

SYDNEY HARBOUR CRUISE

The next day saw us on a harbour cruise. It seems we like to see places from the water. This one was two hours long, with many stops around the harbour.

It was the equivalent of the hop-on-hop-off bus in Singapore, with passengers getting off and on the various docks on the route. We chose to stay on the boat for the entire cruise and enjoy the ride.

We passed underneath the Sydney Harbour Bridge which, when seen from below, is enormous. We could see groups of walkers being led up to the very top of the bridge, which looked a bit scary to us. We did briefly play with the idea of trying that walk, but in the end common sense prevailed!

Our first stop was Darling Harbour where the Aquarium and the Maritime Museum were situated. We docked briefly then it was back to Circular Quay for more passengers. We passed a huge cruise ship docked in the harbour. From our point of view, it looked very unappealing and not for us. Then it was off to Taronga Zoo across the other side of the harbour, where several families left to visit the exotic animals. A gondola from the dock area took visitors up to the zoo. I image the kids must have enjoyed the experience of a boat trip and gondola ride, before enjoying the zoo.

En route we passed the navy docks where several warships were moored. Out in the centre of the channel a sec5ond cruise ship was moored. It was just as big as the one in dock and I wondered just how many passengers are needed to make them profitable. We knew that some cruises had been cancelled due to the Coronavirus, which made us wonder about the economic impact on the cruise lines. A couple we had talked to in Singapore told us their cruise had been cancelled because of the Coronavirus, and what would that cost these companies?

Our next stop was Watson's Bay, a lovely place full of sailboats, cabin cruisers and speedboats. Our ferry was obliged to follow a four-knot speed limit to avoid making waves. We could also see what looked quite like two canoes or kayaks, each with a single paddler. They were maneuvering their craft easily through all the traffic and moored boats. There was also a lovely beach where kids were enjoying the sand and the sea.

Then we made our way past the opening of Sydney Harbour and looked out on the Tasman Sea. There was quite a swell when we left the shelter of the harbour, and we could see huge waves crashing onto the rocks. It was something to think about the ships coming from Europe in the early 19th century, although I am sure people knew about this harbour many years before that.

After passing the entrance to the harbour, our next stop was the Quarantine Station, where any ships with infectious diseases aboard would have to dock first. It looked so peaceful today, but it must have been a busy place so many years ago. (It was ironical to think it could be needed again.)

We passed a buoy with a couple of seals resting on it, which reminded us of the harbour seals we had seen in Alaska doing exactly the same thing. They were not too obliging, as they had hidden under the superstructure! The last stop on the outward trip was a pause at Manly Wharf, a very pretty town with a nice beach, and a very large and rich residential area. We collected more passengers there, and then the return trip began.

The route back was the reverse of our trip out, and as we returned, we picked up passengers along the way. Visiting the entire harbour made us realize just how large it really is, and we were glad we had been able to see it from the water. It really was and amazing experience.

After the harbour tour we walked along the Quay, following the Writer's Walk again, this time covering the entire length. There were about 20 plaques, an eclectic and important mix of writers, all of whose work had some reference to Australia. James Michener, Rudyard Kipling, and Germaine Greer were among the names. Again, we thought how nice it would be if Canadian writers could be recognized in this way.

Now it was time to go shopping! We were off to Alice Springs in the morning, planning to take just hand baggage for ease of travelling. So, another wheelie was in our future. We found a nice one with outside pockets for all those documents which have to be shown time and time again! On the way to the store Bob spotted a street artist, but quite different from others we have seen. He was doing a copy of Michelangelo's 'Creation of Adam' from the Sistine Chapel. It was a beautiful rendition of the fresco. We stopped so Bob could compliment him on his work, and then he told him the story of how he got to see that part of the ceiling, and actually touch it.

ALICE SPRINGS

For our out-and-back visit to the Northern Territories we followed the usual practice of packing the essentials and leaving our large cases in the hotel storage. We were heading first to Alice Springs, which would be a second mini hub for the trip to Uluru. We left Sydney early in the morning. Our flight was at 7:00 a.m. which meant being at the airport by 6:15! The hotel breakfast room didn't open until 7:30, so after a minimal breakfast of tea and an apple in our room, we made our way to the airport by taxi, hoping to find something to eat there. After a good search we found a fast-food outlet, so almond croissants and tea cheered us up no end.

While waiting for our flight we got talking to another passenger who was from the southern USA. He was in construction, working on building communication towers and satellite dishes for U.S. Forces bases. He gets the building done and then the techs come in to install the equipment. As a result, he has worked just about everywhere the US has a base. It was really interesting to chat with him, and during our conversation we learned his home was in Virginia near Chincoteague, where we have camped. He had worked at Wallops Island, near Chincoteague, just one of the launch sites for rockets in the US It must have been a nice posting, near friends and family.

Why is it that time always appears to go so slowly when waiting for that wonderful announcement: 'We are commencing boarding.' This flight was with Qantas, and was very busy aircraft. The plane looked somewhat older than some we have been on. How did we come to that conclusion? We had much more legroom than on any other recent short hop flight! It reminded me of flying in the '60s when it was more luxurious than today. The other bonus of this flight was a reasonable breakfast, which was something we were not used to! It took us about three hours to Alice Springs, and as we began to descend, we saw that the ground was very lumpy with large rocky outcrops, all dry and red, with very scrubby looking bush of a faded green. Not the friendliest of landscapes, and very different from anything we had seen before.

Alice Springs has a very small airport, so when we landed, we came down steps rolled up to the plane, and then crossed the tarmac to the airport buildings. It was hot, much hotter than expected, and the flies descended on everyone. We made our way to the airport shuttle bus which took passengers to the various hotels in Alice Springs. It gave us a short tour of the area during its drop-offs, and a real taste of the very dry earth and scrubby plants.

We checked in to our quite modest motel, but its great advantage was its location right in the centre of Alice Springs. This was important, although we didn't realize it at the time, because the temperature during the day hovered around 35°C! It really was too hot to walk far, but fortunately we were close enough to all the places we wanted to visit and the things we wanted to see.

Our first task was to visit K-Mart (yes, there is one in Alice Springs) and buy some very necessary bug spray and sunscreen, before we could start exploring. In the Tourist Centre we had much discussion about how to get to Uluru, and we decided to book a bus to take us there and back, leaving in a couple of days. This was a tour bus, but our tickets were simple out and back. It's about a four-hour drive, with a couple of stops on the way, so we were looking forward to seeing a lot more of the landscape than we would have done going by plane.

Since this was Sunday, few of the businesses were open, but we did find a pub/restaurant called Uncle's and had veggie burgers, which were very tasty. We thought we'd check out the dry riverbed of the Todd River, which 'flows' through the town, but extremely infrequently. We were told that the people of Alice Springs hold a regatta with boats on wheels, which they push along the dry river bed! We weren't there at the right time for that celebration, but it sounds like a lot of fun, and would be an interesting variation on the ancient tradition of regattas!

By this time, we were learning just how incredibly annoying the flies can be. These nasty little creatures don't bite but are always searching for water. They find people's faces are a good source of this lifegiving fluid, and as soon as you go out, they congregate around your eyes, mouth, nose, and neck; anywhere they can reach moisture. They are awful! We'd tolerated them for a

while, but then we returned to the Visitor Center and bought hats with bug nets! It felt weird wearing these things, although it did make life a lot easier. Mind you, everybody says we will need them when we go to Uluru in a couple of days. While buying our hats, we noticed an advert for an evening camel ride. It sounded intriguing, so naturally we signed up for the following day. Neither of us had ever ridden a camel, so this would be a completely new experience. We were looking forward to finding out just how different it would be from riding a horse.

After our busy day yesterday, we slept in and missed breakfast. Fortunately, Bob was able to go down to the breakfast room and bring a couple of things before they closed. We enjoyed our simple breakfast in our room while planning our day. We were lucky enough to be in Alice Springs when it rained, and it had rained during the night! We wandered down to the Todd River to see if there had been any change in its parched state. The riverbed was still dry, but in just one or two places there were damp spots. It was trying to become a proper river, but not enough water had come down.

We took a walk along one of the bike paths which are on both sides of the river, following nearest one in the direction of the Telegraph Station, not realizing just how far the Telegraph Station was from our starting point. So, after about 45 minutes we turned back and crossed back over the river and started exploring on that side of the river. As we walked, we encountered several little showers, which really pleased the locals and brought down the temperature, but sadly did not lessen the flies. We were thankful for our face nets which protected our faces from the flies, but the flies found our backs, arms, legs, and any other part of us that was exposed

Megafauna Central

To get away from the flies we found refuge in the Megafauna Central, which certainly deserved a visit. It is an exhibition centre devoted to the Miocene period fossils discovered near Alcoota in the 1950s in a wide plain that used to be a large river. The creatures depicted here roamed this area some eight million years ago and were the forerunners of present-day Australian animals. One particularly interesting display featured a range of skulls from 30 million years ago through 20 and 15 million, and into the hundreds of thousands. They showed the evolutionary development of one class of creature in a very graphic way, and very hard to dismiss or explain away by evolution deniers. At the rear of the gallery there was a video presentation of the techniques used by the paleontologists to excavate and preserve the finds.

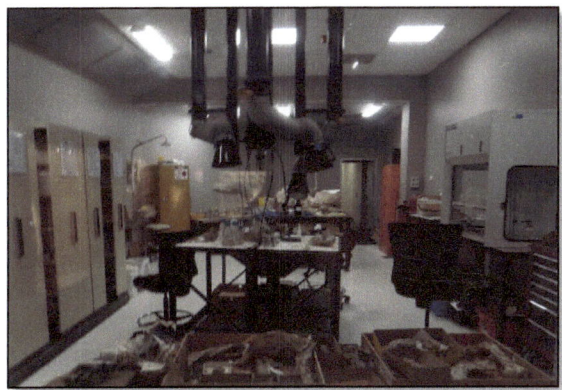

The very well-equipped preparation lab where all specimens are documented and stabilized

The staff member at reception was very helpful in describing the exhibits, and we had a long discussion with her about the treatment of the collection and the functions of the centre in excavating and preserving the finds. She also gave us useful tips about other places to visit.

Then in need of sustenance we found our way to the local shopping mall and had some very nice iced coffees. The young lady behind the counter proved to be very interested in us and Canada. We had a lovely talk about our country, especially the bit about our bugs and the fact that they bite! One day she hopes to visit Canada and probably will.

After that charming interlude we started walking along the bike path once more and noticed something very interesting. There were plaques along the way honouring the Australian military engagements over the last 120 or so years. It also had markers showing the changes in the 'Rising Sun' badge, which has been worn by soldiers of the 1st and 2nd Australian Imperial Force in both world wars. High on the hill overlooking the walk was the Anzac monument for the fallen. It was a very different way of paying homage to their military, and we enjoyed learning a tiny bit more about their history.

In our travels we found the confluence of the Todd and Wright Rivers, which was very dry. It felt very odd to see a confluence in this dry area, and realize that when it rained, it really would be a meeting of the two rivers. We hoped that there would be more rain while we were there so we could actually see it. As we walked back along the river, we saw lots of birds. While we could not identify them it was fun just watching them.

Then it was back to the mall to do some grocery shopping. We have eaten so many meals in restaurants over the last couple of months, nice though that is, there are times we just want a simple and light meal, so cheese, crackers, hummus, and tomatoes made a very nice lunch, finished off with a nice crunchy apple. Then it was time to prepare for our camel ride that evening.

RIDING CAMELS

We were picked up by the camel-ride company and driven out to their farm. On the way we collected several other intrepid people, so we were five in total. The farm is quite a way outside of Alice Springs and took about half an hour to get there. Once there we were introduced to the camels who were all kneeling down, and to get on them we had to climb over the saddle and sit back. So, before we even started the walk, we were given instructions on how to get on and also given information about the animals and how to behave with them. Bob and I were on the same animal, named Selim Mohammad. Once on our camel we leant backwards as he stood up. It was a weird feeling, but we managed to stay on. One by one the others were mounted, then the camels were each attached to the one in front, a camel train. The guide walked in front of the train leading the first camel.

Riding a camel is different from riding a horse and we quickly got used to the movement of the beast and were able to relax into the saddle. Our camel was the last one on the train, and he was obviously bothered by the flies. He kept surging ahead and rubbing his face on the legs of the rider on the camel next in line or, failing that, he used the camel's rump as his itching post.

We were out for about an hour and saw a great deal of the bush and the hills. It was a memorable ride and one I would like to do again. It also gave as an insight as to why these animals were brought over to work as pack animals in Australia. They are strong, can carry large loads and need to drink infrequently because they get most of their fluids from the plants they eat. When they find water, we were told they could drink up to 75 litres at a time! It seems a lot to me, but that's what we were told. After the ride we were driven back to the hotel, tired and at the same time, exhilarated by our experience

That evening, fully recovered from our camel ride we went out to look for supper. It was Sunday and Alice Springs was very quiet. Only one or maybe two places were open, neither of which we fancied. We found a corner store a bought some package soup and crackers and then got talking to the guy behind the cash. He was from Bahrain and temporarily in Australia. He has family in various places including Canada, so we talked about Canada and encouraged him to visit his family in Regina. It was a very pleasant way to end the evening. We went back and enjoyed our soup and crackers and then to bed. We keep on meeting and talking to people on our travels who are interested in learning about Canada. Because we are chatting with so many people, we also learn a great deal about where they come from, and have many interesting conversations.

It poured with rain all that night, so right after breakfast we went down to the Todd River to see what it was like. It was still raining fairly heavily when we set out, but that didn't stop us. On the assumption that it would be hot and dry for this leg of the trip, we hadn't brought jackets! Well, rain or

not, we were going to the river. Besides, the rain kept the flies down and we did have our hats. The transformation from our first day when we had seen a dry riverbed was amazing; lots of muddy red water flowing through one channel, and quite a gusher where a side stream came in. The local people had not seen any water in the Todd for the last 18 months, so we considered ourselves very fortunate to be here right at this time.

Due to the lack of rain gear, our clothes were very wet! Back at the hotel we wondered how to dry them. We were leaving early the following morning to make our way to our hotel in Uluru. Years of camping with those inevitable rainy days helped a lot with that. Spreading this all clothing around on chairs, using hangers for the shirts, turning the A/C up to sauna levels, and running the fan, all helped to dry everything. But living in that 'sauna' was not very comfortable. At one point we escaped and took our computers down to the hotel dining room and spent a very long time on the phone and various websites sorting out our plans for Cairns, Hamilton Island, and the Great Barrier Reef, which was to be our final excursion of this trip.

Museum of Central Australia

It was still raining so in the afternoon we started with the Museum of Central Australia. Because of the rain we enjoyed travelling in the luxury of a taxi. We were amused by our own reaction to the rain. For us rain is normal, but in the dryness of Alice Springs, it was something to enjoy.

The museum houses exhibits of geology, paleontology, and wildlife. A large section was dedicated to meteorites, with plenty of examples and descriptions of where they were found. To demonstrate the inner structure, some of the meteorites had cut and polished sections showing beautiful patterns.

The next set of exhibits dealt with fossils from the earliest examples to almost the present. Australia is famous for its stromatolites, structures produced 3.5 billion years ago by a form of bacteria. They are the earliest known examples of organic life on earth. This was followed by more displays of each of the geological ages, with representative fossils. Then it was on to display cases of taxidermy specimens of a wide range of animals native to Central Australia. All of this was beautifully exhibited and described using the most modern techniques.

Upstairs was a gallery of photographs taken in the early 20th century of life at a Lutheran mission north-west of Alice Springs. Looking at these wonderful pictures we realized just how beautiful black and white photography can be when done really well. There were many depictions of everyday life on the cattle stations, and lots of portraits of both aboriginals and settlers. A very informative and beautiful exhibition.

CENTRAL AUSTRALIAN MUSEUM OF AVIATION

After that most interesting visit, we walked over in the rain to the Central Australian Museum of Aviation. This was quite a contrast to the previous visit, not only with the subject matter but also with the quality of the presentation. It was quite 'amateurish,' but this is not to put it down; it was clearly the work of a great many enthusiastic volunteers, and they had amassed a huge collection of aviation memorabilia. It was all under cover in two large hangars, and clearly treasured and cared for.

The one display we both enjoyed was the Douglas DC-3, a plane that featured large in our experiences of years ago. There was a video presentation set up at the front of the cabin, so visitors could sit in the seats and watch a history of aviation in this area. Seeing the DC-3, reminded me of a trip I took in 1968, aged 10, when the pilot invited me into the cockpit, so I was able to watch where we were going. It also brought back memories for Bob, flying up to the north of Canada in one of these planes in the early 2000s. The real workhorses of that era. After spending some time in this interesting place, the museum staff kindly called a taxi for us, and we were whisked back to our hotel.

Once back at the hotel, we looked for somewhere for supper. We found a nice place, Grill Me Crazy. The name was a bit off-putting but by this time it was the only place available. We went in and met the guys there. It turned out to be a really nice and friendly restaurant. Bob's choice for supper was poutine! Who makes poutine in Alice Springs? We just found someone who did. I just had a quesadilla, which was quite delicious. Together with a glass of wine it made a nice meal. The restaurant staff were fun and were really happy to hear about Canadian poutine and to get a review of their product. The review was positive in the fact there was no gravy on the fries, just lots of melted cheese. Bob thought that an improvement! So, after a nice supper it was back to the motel to get ready for the morning.

Once we were in our room, with all that we had done that day, we had forgotten to tell the motel manager we were leaving the next day. Unfortunately, reception was closed so we had to call the emergency number. After profuse apologies we told him we were leaving very early the next morning but would be back in a couple of days. Our room was already booked, so would it be okay if we paid for everything then? That was agreeable to him, so we relaxed and got ready for our trip to Ayers Rock Resort.

Chapter Ten:
Uluru and Kata Tjuta

We left Alice Springs on the bus at O-dark-early, after a cup of tea and a cookie in our room. (We were leaving too early for breakfast.) This part of the bus journey was one leg of a tour; we had bought tickets for just the outward and return legs. Our first stops were in town picking up travelers from several hotels. Our driver had a public address system and gave us all sorts of information as we traveled. He was incredibly knowledgeable and very witty, and the time passed quickly. This was good because the road was almost dead straight and the scenery very monotonous.

Once out of town we headed south on the Stuart Highway and made our first stop at a roadhouse called Papa Smurf's, on account of the owner's collection of Smurfs, which were happily on display. We told him about the toyboxes with paintings of the Smurfs on the side which Bob had made for the kids years ago, and he was amused. We were told his toasted sandwiches were famous, so we ordered one. Well, it was food and we hadn't had breakfast. The coffee and tea were excellent though. We got chatting to a couple of the other passengers, a retired lady from Barcelona and a lady from Belgium who was going to Uluru to take a job as a tour guide.

The next stop was at Ghan, the junction of the Stuart and Lassiter Highways, where we would turn to head west. We were told the owner kept emus and that we could feed them. The driver did warn us that once the food was finished, they would move away. The roadhouse stop at the junction was packed with people, cars and buses as the Aboriginals were holding a 'Sorry Business' to remember four young people killed in a car accident on Christmas Night.

Buying anything, or even using the washroom, was out of the question, but we did drift over to the pen where emus were kept. We had no food for them because we couldn't get into the store to buy it, so we just leaned over the fence and hoped they would come our way. In a couple of minutes, a flock of them appeared, no doubt thinking we were going to feed them. We were able to photograph them as they came closer, but they must have realized we didn't have food for them, because they gradually veered away.

I was walking back to the coach when I noticed an RV, or caravan as they call them here, and wandered over to talk to the people in it. They were from Germany, traveling through Australia, and right now heading to Uluru. Bob came over and we chatted for a while, talking about traveling around various places. It was a nice interlude in a very busy place.

Back on the road we passed through several cattle stations, each having many hundreds of square kilometers of land. There were signs on the road warning drivers about cattle wandering onto the road. There were few fences in this area which is not surprising given the massive acreage of the stations. At one point we saw cattle just sitting or eating on berms beside the road, and under the shade of the various trees lining the highway. As before the scenery was very monotonous with semi-desert, dunes, and scrubby plants. The driver told us that these dunes are very old; many thousands of years. They are all held together with the massive root systems of all the trees and plants that grow on them. The sand is bright red and relatively fine and barely supports the vegetation growing on it.

One of the trees growing here is the Desert Oak. This is not an oak; it was just called that by the early explorers and settlers. The Anangu peoples know the tree as Kukara. Many of the trees are thought to be perhaps a hundred or more years old. It is difficult to assess as these trees don't have growth rings to count. When the seed is dropped it will grow up and look like a skinny broom with very little canopy. The tap root needs to grow down to find water, which may take many years. Once it reaches the water the canopy begins to grow. Our driver told us the bark is very thick and can protect it from fire. However, when lightning strikes the tree the sap inside the trunk gets overheated and will boil and blow off the canopy!

We made our third stop at a look-off where we could view Mount Connor, the huge mesa of a mountain that is sometimes mistaken for Uluru, or so our driver told us. We also climbed up a sand dune which overlooked a large salt-lake, where we could see the white patches of fresh salt. It was much larger than I expected, although if the truth be known I really didn't know what to expect. Apparently, this stop is known for its 'long dropper.' Everyone seemed to want to check it out! Bob also went to see how it stood up to campground stinkies and came to the conclusion that we could tell them a thing or two about such amenities. Soon after this stop we crossed the border of the Uluru-Kata Tjuta National Park. At this point our driver told us to keep on the lookout for Uluru and the other well-known feature, Kata Tjuta. We were soon able to see them both in the distance.

ULURU-KATA TJUTA NATIONAL PARK

Once we arrived at the Outback Pioneer Lodge, our new home for the next couple of days, we got off the bus and went to check in. Ayers Rock Resort is a beautifully laid out complex of low buildings arranged around a central sand dune. All the buildings were limited by the park authorities to one-storey, so their impact on view lines would be minimal. There are hotels, restaurants, a museum and gallery, a campsite, and service areas all one story high and all very much a natural part of this beautiful place. As soon as we had checked in, gone to our room and had tea (of course), we headed up to the viewing area on the central dune for our first real look at Uluru, 10 kilometers to the south-east. Even at this distance it was quite spectacular. To get there we had to climb the sand dune and walk along the path between Spinifex plants. At the top there is an open area so visitors to the park can see Uluru and Kata Tjuta, both in the far distance. There is a coin telescope, looking very sad and unused. If it's like all the others we've seen like that, it's probably not that good.

Now it was time to take a rest, check up on our email, and catch up with all those electronic chores we needed to do. After which we decided to go up to the dune again at sunset for another look at Uluru. Because we were a fair distance away it did not seem as spectacular as we hoped, but just seeing the sun lighting up one side of it was a gift. After the sun was almost gone, we went down, got rid of the very useful fly nets, and went for dinner at the hotel restaurant, a costly but necessary move. Before settling for the night, we went outside to look at the stars which were spectacular, and after a few disoriented minutes Bob was able to find an upside-down Orion, high overhead instead of down towards the southern horizon. Venus was the brightest he had ever seen it. A very different view of the stars as seen from Canada.

As we settled for the night, we were truly thankful for the fly nets. We had been told in Alice Springs that the flies would be much worse here. They were right! The nets do prevent the flies landing on and around your face, but they still find their way onto the rest of you. Just getting in and out of the coach was fun! We needed to brush off the flies before entering, which was not always successful! Then the A/C in the vehicle calmed them down somewhat as they don't like cool weather, but leaving the coach is a joy for the flies, as they immediately congregate around you looking for any water they could find. Thankfully they don't bite, but they are an annoying nuisance when you are outside! The other positive thing about these beasties is at night they rest up for the morning's attack on unsuspecting people or animals! However, they are only after moisture, which is why they go for the face. I guess this is an adaptation that allows them to live in this environment.

PATJI TOUR OF ULURU

We were collected at our hotel by a four-wheel drive Mercedes van. We had chosen the Patji tour, which was organized and led by the Aboriginal community, because we felt it would give us a deeper experience. Three other people were on the tour with us, retired parents and their daughter from Florida. We were lucky to be on a tour with very few participants because the full capacity of the van was eleven. We drove first in the direction of Uluru, then went about halfway round the rock to the place where we would pick up our Aboriginal guide.

Uluru began as a sandy fan; a scree slope worn down from huge mountains some 450 million years ago. The sea then covered the sand, which was converted by heat and pressure over another 50 million years into sandstone. Fast forward and tilt the strata up 90 degrees and the present formation of arose. Apparently, most of this formation is buried four or five kilometers deep; all we see is the very tip.

The close-up views of Uluru as we drove around it were awesome, but once we were well into our tour, we realized how much more we were getting. Our guide pointed out various parts of the rock and named them for us. He also showed us the damage that had been done to the rock by thousands of tourists over many years. They have actually worn a path up the rock to the top. It looks like an overgrown ant path, and the Aboriginal name for ants, mingas, was also applied to the climbers. You can look as much as you like, and take many photographs, but in the end it's the historical and cultural context that's important, and that's what we were hoping for. We drove through an Aboriginal settlement, out onto dirt roads, and soon passed out of the park and into the Uluru people's traditional land.

Our driver was part-Aboriginal, and had lived in several parts of Australia. From what he said, it seems he had been estranged from his Aboriginal background. Now he wanted to regain that heritage and had come to this area to work and learn about his history. He did tell us that there were so many different Aboriginal family groups in Australia that he didn't know which one he belonged to. But being here in Uluru was helping him regain his ancestral knowledge. He is very happy here and loves working in this area. He says every time he goes out on a tour with guides, he learns more about this place and its Aboriginal history.

Our Aboriginal guide told us about his family and the family group he lives in. His family is Uluru, and they have lived here for generations. This land is his playground and his school and his university. To live in this environment, you must know how to survive in it, and recognize how to find food and water. He would laugh when he said, 'I would skip school and go into the bush, my playground and real school.'

He told us of his love for the land and the traditional ways of his people, and how he had often skipped school to go hunting. Throughout the trip he tried to teach us words in his native language, which we had to repeat but, sadly, they didn't really stick. He spoke of his father and uncles passing down the lore to him, and how he had learned by living off the land. He had a wealth of traditional lore and techniques to show us, so we would stop the van while he collected plants to show us how resourceful the people were. One plant was pounded on a stone to extract the gum that was used to make a glue. Another plant yielded an antiseptic that could be extracted with a little saliva and rubbed into a wound. A dry, grass-like shrub that smelled strongly of camphor when crushed was used to treat colds and fevers. Then there was a bush with berries that could be used as an abortifacient, although it was described as a contraceptive. We were given dried figs, which were quite tasty but would have been better when full of juice.

We stopped for tea at a lean-to hut that had a large water tank on one side. The tank was used to collect rainwater from the roof of the hut. These more modern 'waterholes' were built to keep out the wild camels, who would pollute the waterholes while drinking from them. These tanks were a means of providing travelers with water during their journeys, and our guide was very focused on the importance of water here, as access to it could be the difference between life and death.

During our tea break our guide showed us spears, or throwing sticks, which have a notched end that fits into a 'launcher.' You hold the launcher with the spear hooked on the end and hurl it forward. It takes a lot of practice, as witnessed by Bob's first attempt compared with our guide's. The pointed head of one of the spears had become detached, so we were shown how to repair it. Some gum was extracted from the plant we had been shown, then a fire was lit and the powdered gum picked up on a hot stick, which was rotated in the fire. Meanwhile, the guide was chewing a length of kangaroo Achilles tendon to get it soft and supple. Once enough gum had been gathered on the stick, he heated it in the fire, rotating the stick to avoid dripping, then applied it to the beveled end of the spear. The spearhead was pressed into place, a little more heat applied, and then the kangaroo tendon was wrapped tightly around. Once the tendon dried, it would shrink and bind the spearhead tightly to the shaft.

Repairing the damaged spear using natural resin and tendon

After our tea we were given a presentation about the treatment of the Aboriginal people by the white settlers. This was a no-holds-barred account of chains, hunting and execution, punishment for taking cattle that had strayed onto 'their' land from a nearby station. Our guide passed around pictures of his relatives who had escaped punishment by splitting up and running in different directions. He described forcible removal of children, attempts at assimilation, and the horrible fact that as late as the early 20th century the Aborigines were not even considered legally human! Our guide showed us the family trees of the Uluru people going back five generations and described the efforts of the present generation to cement the Aborigine's place in modern Australia. All of this, of course, was familiar to us, and the stories could be transposed to Canada with scarcely any change. Everywhere we go we encounter the damage that colonialism did and see how it reverberates down the generations. The young children learn this history and it is passed on. 'Even now, we don't know whether to trust the white man.' And who can blame them?

We stopped at a 'rock hole' where ground water would well up, although this one was dry. It was fenced around to prevent wild camels from drinking because they made it unfit for consumption and prevented other animals from using it. Knowing where these water sources were located was critical to survival in the Outback.

Honey ants live in nests deep underground. It wasn't possible to show us how the honey was extracted because the digging often takes several hours. Our guide recalled being taken out into the bush when he wanted to be playing with his friends, and spending hours digging down about five feet into the nest. The reward for the labour was the honey. It would have been great to see how the honey was made, but he did show us pictures of some very bulbous and shiny ants.

Our stop for lunch was 'interesting' on account of our friends the flies. We found out how nearly impossible it was to have a picnic lunch without adding a great deal of fly protein to the meal! We were told in Alice that if you think the flies are bad here, wait 'til you get to Uluru. Very true. The food was soon dense with them, so to make a chicken and salad wrap, one person would wave over the food like a semaphore signal while the other quickly slapped the contents on. An added complication was the nets over our faces; you had to pull the net up quickly, stuff the food in, and swiftly pull it down. There was a temptation to drink our soft drinks through the mesh.

After lunch we parted company with our guide, and our driver took us back to our hotels. At the tourist office we made bookings for a tour to Kata Tjuta the next day. We had seen Kata Tjuta from a distance, and it looked wonderful, so with the booking made we went back to our room, discussing all we had seen and learned that day. One of the things we pondered was all the other historical monuments and buildings we have seen with their worn steps from millions of people visiting over many, many years. We compared them to the worn pattern of those who climbed Ayers Rock, as it was called then, and realized that the pathway these 'mingas' had made was a completely different thing. Wearing of stone because a building is in use over time—perhaps a church or mosque where people come to pray—is very different from the tourist idea of 'Been there, done that.' The worn pathway at Uluru was not religious in origin, but rather a statement of our ability to visit things, climb things, and sometimes take souvenirs of things, just because we can.

We started to understand why the Aboriginal people of this land were upset with all those people climbing the rock for no good reason. As our guide said, 'How would you like it if we came and climbed all over the Vatican?' A very good point, and much food for thought.

KATA TJUTA

Before our visit to Kata Tjuta, we checked out the gift store in our hotel complex. There were many typical Uluru-focused items aimed at tourists, such as hats, mugs T-shirts and so. The universal tackiness found anywhere in the world. There were a couple of interesting items of indigenous artwork, and, although lovely, we wondered how many times these items had been marked up every time they move up the marketing chain! I am sure the artist got a minimal payment.

Kata Tjuta means 'many heads' in the local language, which its shape makes most appropriate. Our van came at 2:30 and we were the last to get on board. It was crowded with nine other people and we were at the back, not the nice restful tour we had to Uluru. The drive to Kata Tjuta took us into the National Park, so we had to buy day passes before being allowed in. We didn't realize this because yesterday was the Patji tour and we didn't need them as our driver and guide were aboriginal, but today was a regular tour which meant passes were necessary. This was a much longer drive, some 45 km, and our driver Julia covered the distance to the far side of the rocks in record time. Unfortunately, it meant there were no opportunities to take pictures on the way there, as the van was just going too fast. We were assuming there would be an opportunity on the way back.

Before we started our trail walk among the rocks, we were offered extra water if we needed it; we didn't but some others filled their bottles. Our guide gathered us around under a shelter and, using a stick to draw diagrams in the dust, showed how the rocks had been formed. This crude method was used very effectively; we understood that Kata Tjuta began as a rocky fan – a scree slope – eroded from vast mountains worn down 450 million years ago, unlike Uluru, which began as sand. The sea then covered the debris, which was converted by heat and pressure over another 50 million years into a conglomerate. The strata then tilted up at about 15 degrees and the formation we were looking at arose. Like Uluru, most of this formation is buried four or five kilometers deep.

The walk was described as two kilometers out and back. We started on a gravel path heading into a deep cleft, or gorge, between two hills, but soon found out it wasn't a nice easy path. We had to climb over rocky conglomerate, smooth but hardly even. The rock under our feet was composed of rounded pebbles cemented together, with the occasional loose boulder detached from the sides of the gorge. Erosion took place mostly on the shaded side of the hills because this is where the freeze/thaw cycle takes place. We were surprised to learn that it did get below freezing occasionally here. We continued up the path and into the gorge, stumbling over these 'blasted boulders,' occasionally coming to bridges built across deep clefts that ran across our path. Vegetation clung to areas where water ran, and it was amazingly bright in colour. This was a hike like no other that we have taken.

Interestingly, we could see that, just like Uluru, a path was being created by the thousands of feet walking along it, which now included ours. Because of all we had leant the previous day, it made us wonder how the Aboriginal community felt about this, as Kata Tjuta also has religious significance.

The heat was baking by now, somewhere in the mid-30s and it was very dry. We sought any tiny bit of shade we could find, as well as drinking much of our water. Occasionally, our guide would stop and provide information on the types of plants and the formation of the rocks. The last part of the walk looked more challenging, so Bob and I turned around and waited while the group completed the last couple of hundred metres. After a short while we slowly started back, and about halfway through our return journey they reeled us in. Julia was over-solicitous, even though we insisted that everything was fine; we were slow but perfectly capable. Nevertheless, when we got back to the van, she insisted on dissolving some rehydration salts into our water bottles. Delicious! Frozen wet flannels in Ziploc bags were distributed to everybody, which we all appreciated. We did ask if we would be stopping for a photo-op on the way back, but we were told there wouldn't be time. We were sorry about this because it would have made this interesting hike so much better. To be able to view this formation close enough to see as many of its 13 peaks as possible would have been a great experience. Finally, we were dropped off at our hotel and because we had been picked up last, it was our fate to be dropped off at last! It had been a fascinating journey and we were very happy to see have seen some of Kata Tju̱ta, but a little dissatisfied at the lack of time in the schedule.

The Field of Light

At 8:30 in the evening we were picked up for a visit to the Field of Light. A full-sized bus appeared and then did the rounds of the other hotels and the campsite until it was nearly full. We were led from the bus down a path that was marked each side with low-level lights. The Field of Light consists of thousands of 'hand-blown' glass globes with LED lights inside, which change colour gradually in a way we're very familiar with. There are paths between the sections of the field so you can walk among the lights. Our main takeaway from this experience was that a viewer could only really appreciate the effect from above; at ground level it was just a great mass of beautiful lights. As we walked around, it was possible to appreciate the changing colours of the lights, but it was not possible to see how the patterns of the lights changed since we were at their level. If there had been a viewing platform it would have been so much better. Without an idea of the overall pattern and size of the installation, we have to say that the experience was underwhelming.

One side benefit of being away from the lights around the hotel area was the night sky. Even with a gibbous moon high in the sky, it was still possible to make out the Milky Way and the Great Nebula in Orion. What it must be like without the moon can only be imagined. The Southern Cross was easily visible, which was a nice indication of how far around the world we were.

Return to Alice Springs

Our bus for Alice Springs left at 12:30, so there was time for a slow start to the day. We were working away at our packing when the front desk phoned us, reminding us that to check-out was 10:00 a.m., and it was now 10:30! Oops, didn't read the small print! We quickly packed up everything and made our way to the reception area in the main building of the hotel to wait for the bus. We had a tour of the entire resort and the bus picked up passengers from the other hotels, before starting the drive back to Alice.

Once out of the National Park and across a cattle grid we were on the land of the Curtin cattle station. This is one of the largest in this area at over one million acres. There's an interesting story about this station: when Peter Severin came up here in 1956, he was married and had a young baby. According to legend, he didn't tell his wife what he was planning before he came, and only told her when they arrived. It is said that he would not let her have the car keys for six months because she would drive back south and leave him there. They lived under a tree for the first few months until they built a house. The cattle station has flourished, and the family has welcomed people to their home since their arrival in this area. Apparently, his wife made wonderful scones and people coming in were welcomed with the scones, jam, and cream. Now there is a restaurant, a campground, and a little store. The station is run by Peter's son, with help from Peter who is now in his 90s. The family owns some of the land of the station, and the rest is leased from the government. Mount Connor is on the land they own and can be visited by arranged tours.

We had a brief stop at the restaurant, and enjoyed a couple of muffins, not scones, which were advertised as fresh baked and not from a package. We were tempted by the bottles of Fucking Great Port on sale at the store, but it wasn't very practical with all the travelling we still had to do, and it might have taken us a while to drink it all. We just took a picture (which is filed, not printed here). Trevor, the man behind the counter, said they sent it anywhere in the world, so Bob slipped their business card into his pocket.

Back on the bus we headed down to the junction for Kings Canyon. We had noticed the transfer point on our way to Uluru, so we weren't surprised at this extra stop on our way. Some of the passengers were going to Kings Canyon—which is apparently another spectacular geological site—and transferred to another bus. The bus door was left open for long periods, so the flies hitched a ride! A lady in the seat opposite us kept swiping them away from her window. No sooner had she swiped one mass away, another group would form. This went on for most of the trip, and I was amazed at her ability to keep doing this as well as her intolerance! And, of course, the futility of the enterprise.

The return journey was very similar to the drive down except this time we saw more cows. They were well hidden in the bush, so they would flash past before I could get the camera out. We stopped at Erldunda, where the emus were. It was much less busy this time, so we were actually able to buy some emu food and feed them. There were a lot more of them this time, and they were clustered around the feeding area. They are huge birds with very nasty looking beaks. We put the food on the flat top of the fence and the birds went nuts, pushing and shoving for the pellets. No sense of manners at all! It didn't take long before the food was gone, but they still begged for more. All too soon it was back on the bus, a left turn onto the Stuart Highway, and the drive straight through to Alice.

Again, the road was very similar: straight, lots of scrubland, dunes, and dry riverbeds. Our driver told us about the Royal Flying Doctor Service, which is part of Australia's Healthcare System, and the School of the Air, a radio broadcast which is the only and maybe best way to teach the children living on the cattle stations, and whose nearest neighbours could be a hundred kilometres away! We crossed the Finke River, which is said to be the oldest in the world. It has been flowing in that bed for millions of years. Ironically, it was dry when we drove over it.

One of the interesting facts our guide told us: Qantas is one of the oldest airlines in the world, and its name is an acronym of Queensland and Northern Territory Airline Service. We had always wondered why there was no U following the Q. So now we know.

Even though we arrived late in Alice, the hotel desk was still open. We checked in and then went off for supper at Grill Me Crazy. They were busier this evening, so we had to wait for our meal. We got talking to the couple next to us. They were in Alice Springs for the weekend; they come most weekends to have a break from their work in an isolated village. She is a teacher and he is the school handyman. The school, St Theresa's Catholic School is in an aboriginal village down a gravel road, about 20 or 30 km away. They enjoy working there and find that a break on weekends refreshes them. They are from India and have family all over the place, including Canada. It was lovely to talk with them while we all waited for our food. This time Bob had pulled pork poutine, which he found very tasty, but true poutine it wasn't. The gentleman we were talking to also had the pulled pork poutine, so we explained it was a French-Canadian dish and should have cheese curds as well as gravy with the fries.

After supper it was time to go back to the hotel and bed. Here comes the silly bit. I had seen the hotel key card on the dresser. I asked Bob if he had one. Yes, okay. Well, he pulled out his 'key card' and found it was actually the Fucking Great Port business card, that had only felt like a key! Oh well, we will have to disturb the manager again. We got to the hotel and found another guest who had also left his key card in his room! Now there were three of us. The buttons on the outside phone didn't work, which was frustrating, but eventually the manager appeared. How he knew we were there we don't know. He did not look happy. He let us in, gave out the key cards, and we went to our room and to bed.

We had some flight bookings to Cairns and the Great Barrier Reef to confirm the next morning before flying back to Sydney, so we sat down in the breakfast room. While working on the web we noticed on the TV that the Formula One circus was coming to Melbourne for the opening race of the season. Our flights back to Sydney were routed through Melbourne, so while we had no intention of attending the race, it was interesting to speculate on the huge cost of shipping all that equipment halfway round the world.

News of the Formula One arrival would prove to be ominous.

Chapter Eleven:
New South Wales and Victoria

We arrived very early for our flight to Melbourne, which gave us time step out of the airport lounge into an enclosed outside area, where we could take pictures of some older planes, which had been 'mothballed' at the airport. The climate at Alice Springs is perfect for storage: it's dry and has very low humidity because it rains only a few days a year. It is likely they close the planes completely, coat everything that needs coating with oil, wax or grease, and then seal them up. It is a good source of income for the airport, and if the planes are needed again, they can be easily restored to service.

In the departure area near the check-in there was a magnificent 1930s Rolls-Royce airline service truck on display in a glass case, courtesy of the aviation museum we had visited earlier

The plane to Melbourne was scarcely half full, so we had room to stretch out a bit. As on previous relatively short Qantas flights, we were served food, this time some delicious little hot pies. The flight was highlighted by views from the window of the Simpson Desert and a great salt-lake, probably Lake Eyre.

We also spotted an exactly circular salt-lake and wondered if it was a meteor crater. At one point the airline staff called us all to look out of the windows on the right side—which was our side—as we were passing right over Maree Man, a huge figure 4.2 km

long carved into the desert floor, but nobody knows by whom. The local cattlemen, miners, and Aborigines all deny making it, but the light plane and helicopter owners think it's a great idea and would like to 'Buy the bastard a beer.' It's a mystery.

The transfer to the plane for Sydney was problem-free, and again we were served a meal on a flight of scarcely two hours. The view over Sydney Harbour as we came in to land was spectacular.

There was no one waiting for a taxi outside the airport, so the trip continued to be quick and easy. We were thankful we had decided to travel light, leaving the bulk of our luggage at the hotel in Sydney. We arrived at the Sir Stamford hotel—and yes, he is the Raffles one—retrieved our bulk luggage from storage, and started planning the next leg of our journey.

Our chores had been somewhat neglected while we were away, although blogging and maintaining the journal continued, of course. We spent a whole morning getting things sorted out and up to date, then decided to do some exploring.

THE OPAL MUSEUM

This was an amazing place. I knew very little about opals, except that family lore said they were unlucky. We went up an escalator from street level and entered a museum display. The first display case contained fossils that were composed of opal, and quite beautiful to look at. The organic material on these sea creatures had been totally replaced by opal, which gave them a beautiful nacreous appearance. In one display, a dinosaur stepped right out.

Working around the displays we came to dinosaur bones of opal, more sea shells, and some great chunks of the raw mineral. One display case, set into a vault with the door swung open beside it, contained what was described as the largest opal ever discovered. There were two others in the case, smaller but equally gorgeous. The larger part of the 'museum' was devoted to display cases of jewelry on sale. There were earrings, pendants, rings, and bracelets set in gold and silver, all absolutely gorgeous but all far above our budget. One pair of earrings with tiny opals set in them fetched $180.00. However, we had clipped a coupon out of the tourist magazine in the hotel so we received a gift of a pin with a tiny opal set in it.

The Royal Bank of Canada

As our bank's website described twenty-four/seven opening hours, we felt it would be easier and cheaper to withdraw from an ATM rather than paying transaction fees. After much searching, we eventually found the building where the bank was reputedly to be located. It was apparently in the office tower above the shopping mall we were in, and on the top floor no less. We took the elevator to the 47th floor, with nobody questioning us, and walked into the RBC office. 'How come they let you up?' the receptionist asked. We told her that nobody had stopped us! She told us, much to our surprise, that RBC didn't do personal banking in Australia, so we then told her how erroneous the website was. She hilariously told us she would pass our comments along. Afterwards, we realized that we had followed an employee into the elevator at floor level, which was probably how we got up to the bank so easily. Undaunted, we stopped for crepes in another Breton outfit in the ground floor plaza of the building.

St Mary's Cathedral

We continued a walk that took us to Hyde Park, a very pleasant space in the middle of the city's bustle. As we walked through, we came to a lovely fountain and then the cathedral, the mother church of Australian Catholics.

The building, in the Neo-Gothic style, was started in 1866 not long after the previous church had burned down. It took nearly 75 years before it was finished. Even then, the twin spires were not included due to lack of funds; they were finally added in 2000. The interior was very beautifully lit by using yellow/orange glass in the upper windows of the nave, thus giving a lovely warm glow. The artworks around the aisles depicting the stations of the cross were very well done.

We had debated visiting the crypt, but I insisted, and I was very glad I had because it was very rewarding. It was cleared out and renovated in the late 1940s as a resting place for the remains of the previous bishops. The floor was decorated with terrazzo tiles following the Celtic Christian designs seen in the Book of Kells. The detailing and colour of the tiles were beautiful, and the overall effect was astounding. There were also some very finely produced paintings, the most intriguing of which, depicting the Resurrection, was done in a very Salvador Dali style.

THE MUSEUM OF SYDNEY

Over the course of our wanderings, we had passed the Museum of Sydney a couple of times, so we decided to drop in and see what it had on offer. It is a modern glass building on three levels with displays concentrating on the history of the city. Through glass panels set into the lower floor visitors can see the foundations of the original Government House, built at the turn of the 18th century, and demolished in the 1840s. Finds from the archaeological dig were also displayed, and we got the impression that those early settlers smashed an awful lot of crockery! Maybe it was party time in Government House! Seriously, it did show the contemporary pottery and china in use, all of which had been shipped over from England and likely other places in Europe. Most interesting was the model of the original Government House and the various contemporary illustrations used to reconstruct how it must have looked. On that same floor was a fleet of ship models, each representing the type craft that had supplied the early colony, with descriptions of their specifications and cargoes. At this point, one of those strange coincidences took place: we began talking to a lady who was looking at the displays, and it turned out she was from Prince Edward Island and she and Bob had mutual acquaintances in the museum world!

Upstairs another level was a display of photographs of weird architecture from around the world. Well, some like the Taj Mahal weren't weird, but others were quite bizarre. The photographer had chosen strange subjects and done a great deal of work on the images. It was very interesting in its way, but it left us a little flat. There was a large children's area on this floor with all sorts of educational toys available. Along the middle of the gallery a series of posters outlined the history of Sydney with illustrations from many periods of the lifestyle and surroundings.

Back down on Circular Key, we went into a convenience store and bought some hummus, cheese, and cookies for our lunch. By this time on our journey, I was so looking forward to getting back to my own kitchen and ordinary food! Catered food is very nice, and we had some wonderful meals, but sometimes we really just wanted to open a can of soup for lunch! On the way back to our hotel we noticed the nearby Crime and Police Museum and thought it would be interesting to visit but it was only open on weekends. And we thought crime never took a holiday! Since we were planning a road trip, we added it to our list of things to do in Sydney when we came back.

That afternoon we took a taxi to visit Bob's trumpet colleague John Foster who lives in Newtown, not far away. An afternoon was spent in trumpet-talk with periodic blasts of musical fragments. John has a vast collection of trumpets and trumpet-related instruments, many of which were taken out of their display cases and oohed and aahed over. John kindly gave Bob his latest book and some CDs, and Bob gave him a copy of *Making a Natural Trumpet* and signed it for him. Then we Ubered back the hotel, to prepare for our road trip the following morning.

NEW SOUTH WALES

We had a rental car booked at the airport. The car company had no maps at all, and none of the other stores in the airport concourse could help us, so we headed out on the M5 towards Canberra and Melbourne and hoped for the best. The driving was the usual intown expressway driving, with one difference: the police here absolutely do not tolerate speeding, so it is important to keep to the speed limit. There is no grace speed. If you are over the limit and they catch you, that's it! It's a big fine and loss of points. Not sure how that would work with out-of-country licences, but we didn't want to find out. Gradually, as we drove out of town the traffic increased as did the speed limit. It went up from 100 to 110 kph. We pulled in to a rest stop to look for a map, with no success, so we continued down the highway for some time before stopping a second time. We were in no hurry, so a bathroom break, a drink stop, and map search were just part of the trip.

We started seeing roadside billboards for wineries, so after passing several we finally gave in to temptation and stopped at Eling Forest. We had a lovely time tasting a couple of wines and talking to the sommelier. She was from Upper New York State and knew a bit about wines we knew from the Niagara Peninsula. We have enjoyed several wine tasting trips to Niagara, and it was a pleasure talking about familiar territory. She asked all the right questions and we chatted while we were checking out the produce. It was impossible to leave without buying, so we bought one bottle to share with our friends, and a half bottle to share with each other after we stopped for the day. It was a lovely interlude with which to break up the journey.

Our next stop saw us at roadside stall which had a variety of beautiful fruits on sale. We bought cherries and mangos from their wide selection. There were lovely boxes of mixed fruits which made me wish for our RV; it was one of those things we would love to have had on many of our trips. But today, just enough for one day.

After we had been travelling for about four hours it was time to stop for a stretch of legs, etc. In the rest stop store we found some candies, which we were sorely lacking, and Bob finally found the maps he needed to find our way around. We went on our way in a very good mood. We were now driving though an area with many cattle and sheep farms. The cattle were in beautiful green fields enjoying what looked like lush green grass, very different from the scrub we had seen the cattle grazing on the stations in the Northern Territory. Those cattle were left to wander around the stations, and there were fewer head to an acre, while the cattle we saw today had much less space but what looked like a higher quality of food. I don't think I saw even one of the sheep with its head up; they were all munching the grass as if it was all they wanted to do!

The scenery we drove through reminded us of Pennsylvania, with the road passing through forest, relatively low mountains and farms. It was weird being so oddly familiar and yet oddly different. The trees were mainly hardwood rather than pine, but it felt 'normal.' This area has lots of rolling hills so we were up and down them quite frequently and looking into the far distance we could see them row upon row, with only a few towns on the edges of the road.

Finally, we were both tired and it was getting to be time to stop, so we started looking for a motel. We had driven through one area with lots of motels and hotels, but just wanted to go a little further. After a while we were wondering if we had made a big mistake. Then we saw a billboard for the Halfway Motel at Tarcutta. We thought that sounded hopeful and started looking out for the turnoff. We had almost given up, when we saw it. We turned off and found the place not far from the highway. It did not look so promising from the outside, but we were tired, and here we were. The owners were very friendly, and we quickly checked in and found our room. Our neighbour from the next unit was sitting outside, so we started chatting, and a bit later the neighbour on the other side came in and joined us. All in all, it was a very social evening. We ordered supper, the owners brought it to our unit, so we sat outside in the fresh air and ate with the accompaniment of a half bottle of wine we had bought earlier in the day.

All through this meal the birds gave us a wonderful show: parrots, cockatoos and some unidentified bright red ones were calling and flying into the trees and bushes around us. It was a beautiful sight and a wonderful way to end our day. Those same birds made sure we were up early in the morning, and heralded us breakfast. Before heading on our way again, we had to finding the local gas station. Bob had some difficulty in opening the gas tank and the lady at the gas station eventually found the button, which was on the door sill on the driver's side. Whatever made the manufacturers think that was a good place? The gas station lady said this is a big problem with the new cars; many people have difficulty in finding the right button to press or lever to pull. The most ridiculous one she had found was hidden in the armrest! One just wonders why.

Once the gas was sorted out, we headed towards King Valley for some more wine tasting and very prudent buying, mainly as gifts for all our friends here. It was about a three-hour drive, which was not too long for Bob, the sole driver. We were amazed at the number of ranches we passed on both sides of the road. They seemed to alternate between sheep and cows. These are very large spreads with an equivalent number of animals. The scenery was lovely, and apart from the ranches, we saw lots of hills and mountains all around us, lots of nice-looking towns and villages off the main highway, and generally a very tranquil drive.

On thing we found interesting was the freeway design. The main road ran pretty straight through the countryside, so the towns were bypassed by the creation of approximately half-moon shape, which left the highway, skirted the town, and rejoined several kilometers further. It struck me as a practical way to keep the various towns in touch with the rest of the world, yet not have them bothered by the traffic.

We found the direction sign for King Valley and the wineries. To get there we came off the highway, and made our way south among lots more cows and sheep! One thing amused us: the cows were sometimes in a pasture right next to the vineyards! I'm not sure what that did for the terroir. The first winery we came to was closed, so we moved on to the next one. Not as easy as in Niagara as these wineries were several kilometers from each other along a winding road. The second winery was La Cantina, Italian-based with half their grapes originating in Italy. The wines were all well made, and we bought one bottle to take with us.

The next stop was Gracebrook, where we had lunch. The staff were very helpful in accommodating my dietary needs. We had a tasting to see what wine we would like to have for lunch. Or, at least, I did because Bob was doing the driving and the police are very vigilant. He did have a couple of sips. We chose a sauvignon, which was fruity and nicely dry, so we enjoyed a glass with lunch. The tasting bar was a huge plank cut from a very large gum tree. It was quite beautiful and we both admired it. All that remained of the tree was the overturned stump and it was enormous. It was slowly weathering away outside the winery while becoming a talking point for guests. The building itself was reported to be from the late 19th century and had all its original woodwork. The roof had to be redone, but apart from that it seems the main building was authentic.

Lunch was deep-fried zucchini flowers for me, and trout for Bob, both served with salad and bread. After lunch we decided to drive over the mountain to Mansfield. The road is winding and narrow and goes through forested areas. It was an interesting drive especially when we took a diversion to Power's Point, a three-kilometer drive on a dirt road. Fortunately, it was a good dirt road with few potholes and other obstructions. At the end of the road, we came to a lookoff that had a wonderful view over the valley. There was also a walk, up and down rock steps as well as proper metal stairs. It was a challenging walk amongst the rocks, but well worth it at the end. According to a poster at the start of the walk, the gentleman who lent his name to this spot was a fugitive and criminal!

Once back in the car we found our way up and down the mountain, around the curves—what became of all the straight pieces of road?—until we finally found ourselves in Mansfield. We went to the tourist information building to ask about accommodation, but it was closed. We lucked-out because about 200 metres down the road was a motel, where we signed in for the night. Now came the fun bit. There is virtually no internet in this region, which we didn't know until we tried to log-on. Ultimately, Bob went to the motel office where he was able to connect, and then found he was locked in! The owner had to go and collect her kids and had left him inside! Another guest with internet problems came up to tell me she had seen him in there through the window, so I shouldn't worry. By the time I went to the office the owner was back, the door was unlocked, and Bob was free. A little while later the owner knocked on our door and presented us with a bottle of wine as an apology for locking him in! That was our second apologetic bottle of wine on this trip!

The following morning, we had a unique breakfast experience. We had to place our orders the night before, and the meal was delivered some point during the night through a hatch from outside. The bread had to be toasted, the cereal was already in the bowls, and the milk was in jugs. Just toast the bread, add milk to the cereal, open the orange juice and it was ready! A very different breakfast experience, but it worked and was a satisfactory meal. After we had enjoyed this unusual service, we left the motel and started heading to the Yarra Valley wine region.

The drive was similar to the previous day's, with lots of spreads of dairy or sheep, nice rolling hills, and all very pleasant on the eye. Gradually vineyards started showing up until we were passing wineries on both sides of the road. Now came the dilemma: where do we stop? We had no idea which to choose. We finally stopped at a small winery called St Hubert's. We chose it because the brochure said it was possible to have lunch under the oak tree: a glass of wine and a cheese plate. That sounded good to us; Bob would eat the cheese and I would drink the wine with my hummus. Well, like all great plans it didn't turn out that way. The winery was no longer licensed to serve wine outside the tasting area. So, no cheese and no wine. We did try some of their wines and came out with a rather nice Cabernet Sauvignon. And we did have our picnic lunch outside with orange juice not wine. It was quite satisfactory and when finished we went on our way.

HEALESVILLE WILDLIFE SANCTUARY

We had noticed the wildlife sanctuary on our map of the wineries. Since we still haven't seen any Australian wildlife other than roadkill, we decided to pay a visit to the local fauna. The sanctuary was about a half hour drive with lots of road construction cones along the way, which slowed us down a bit. We paid what we thought was a rather high entry fee and entered a beautiful park. It was well laid out with paths, a winding stream, lots of large enclosures and

We saw kangaroos, wallabies, koalas (this little guy on the right), dingoes, echidnas, emus (we fed them lettuce out of a bowl), pelicans and lots of other birds.

The echidna is a crazy creature: a marsupial with porcupine-looking quills, and back legs that face the wrong way for most animals, but work for them. And, of course, there was the world's silliest beast, the duck billed platypus! It was in a large aquarium tank in a darkened area and it was going crazy just swimming around. We didn't know whether this was normal or not. But seeing it was unreal.

Hardly a flattering view, but there you go

There is an aboriginee legend about the duck-billed platypus. In brief:

> A water rat invited a swan to live with him. She stayed a while but then left and went back home. When nesting time came, she was amazed at the babies that hatched from her eggs. They had bills and webbed feet like a duck, four legs instead of two and fur instead of feathers. Everyone was scared of them, so the swan took them upstream so nobody could see them. And that's how the platypus came to be.

When you actually see one, it all makes sense. After a good walk around, it was time to find somewhere to stay for the night.

COVID REARS ITS HEAD

We left the nice rural roads and began to get into traffic. By now we were in the outskirts of Melbourne, it was rush-hour, and then it started to rain very heavily! Not a nice trip at all. We found the Sage Hotel in Ringwood (after driving around it twice and messing around in an endless underground parking lot with poor signage), but it was a lovely hotel and no more expensive than some of the motels we had checked out. We would stay there for two nights to catch up with things and rest a bit; it had been a very busy time since we left Sydney.

The hotel was built on top of a shopping mall, with easy access to the shops below. So, during our rest day, every two hours or so we would go downstairs and walk around the mall, not buying anything, but just being those annoying seniors doing mall walking! We did stop at Woolworths for some cheese, hummus, and crackers for lunches on the road, and some apples and cookies made it into the basket as well.

We were tired of restaurant food, so we went to the food court and bought nice chicken salads and other tasty items for our supper. These, with the juice that the hotel reception desk provided for free, made for a very tasty dinner. The TV news channels were showing nothing but the Corona virus, and by now we realized that the whole issue was getting serious. We had heard of the virus while still in London, encountered it more seriously in India and Thailand, and now it was making itself felt worldwide. Then came the news that the Formula One race in Melbourne was cancelled! Having seen the whole circus arriving on TV when we were in Alice Springs, it was confirmation of how serious this Corona virus was. If that multi-million-dollar enterprise was folding up, the news was dire indeed.

In the morning, with all the TV news about borders being shut and airlines cancelling flights, we completed the on-line registration form for Canadian citizens travelling abroad. We also emailed our friend in Canberra to see if he had further information or at least could get it. He was very helpful and sent us some links with forms to complete. Our son in Canada also sent us information and links to check out. We realized we would need to talk to Air Canada and Aeroplan, but when we tried, their lines were jammed and there was no hope of contacting them. Neither organization would even put a caller on hold at that point, which was actually a good thing; I can just imagine our Bell bill if we had been on hold indefinitely. By this time, it was getting close to checkout time so we gave up, left the hotel and started on the road to visit our friends in Pambula.

DRIVING TO PAMBULA

Our next destination was Pambula where we were to meet our friends Pat and Mike, whom we had known in London 50 years ago. We back-tracked for a little while and then headed east up the Yarra Valley. Beyond the agricultural area the road became all bends and twists going up and down through forests of massive trees. Very beautiful but tough driving. Finally, after about half an hour of forest, we turned south and came out of the trees and into nice countryside and reasonable roads. It was dairy farms with some sheep, huge spreads of land that seem to grow mainly hay for fodder.

Then it was straight on along the Princes Highway with lots of stops and starts as this road goes through towns, not round them. We came to Lakes Entrance where we got the first glimpse of the Tasman Sea, and here we settled for the night at a Comfort Inn, strangely feeling just like home. We left Lake's Entrance the next day and headed to Pambula. The road was very winding and up and down and through forests. Eventually we found some more bucolic areas with lots of cows. I swear we have seen over a million cows during this trip, they are everywhere! The road also goes through many small towns with several traffic lights before it opens up to arable land or forests. Not really a bad drive, but it did get a bit monotonous.

At the halfway point of the drive, we got into the forests ravaged by wildfires. The burn area went on for more than 100 kilometers! It was quite desolate and horrid to see, but we did notice how quickly vines were creeping up the burnt trunks and becoming established. At various points there were workers with heavy machinery cleaning up the sides of the roads, collecting and debarking large trees, which were likely taken to lumber mills. We saw several trucks carrying these logs to wherever.

Finally, we found Pambula and the Airbnb that Pat and Mike had rented. We were there first and were able to explore the outside of the properly. We noticed a number of droppings all over the grass and Bob thought they might be kangaroo, so maybe we would actually see some here. Pat and Mike arrived a little while later and we had a wonderful reunion. It was great to see them again after half a century. We spent time talking and eating lunch and just catching up. After a while we went for a walk along the beach, which was lovely. It was warm and the sound and smell of the sea was wonderful. Once we came home, we enjoyed drinks looking out over the sea. Supper was barbequed chicken with salad—so nice to have a home-cooked meal after so long—and we enjoyed the wine from St Hubert's.

A pair of kangaroos appeared in the garden, grazing on the lawn. Mike said he thought they were a mother and a half-grown joey. We took lots of pictures and sent them off to the kids. Later that afternoon we were looking through the big picture windows when nine kangaroos appeared out there! Two of them came up to the balcony, and it looked as if they were begging, so Mike brought bread out and tried to feed them. They took the food but didn't eat it. Just watching them on the grass keeping the lawn mown down and hopping around was quite wonderful. We hoped they would be back tomorrow. Now we could say we had seen kangaroos in the wild, or perhaps on the lawn!

After supper we sat and caught up with all the family gossip. We had heard, of course, about the destruction of Pat and Mike's house in Mallacoota during the wildfires. They told us all the issues with the fire, and how things were going with the planned rebuild. We discussed our Australian plans and the issue with Corona. We still couldn't get in touch with Aeroplan or Air Canada, and with no WiFi in the house we would have to wait until we got to Canberra.

We watched a movie Pat and Mike had made about Mallacoota. It is a totally beautiful place, and it is very sad to think about the effects of the wildfires. They were both upbeat about the situation, although I was sure there are times when it feels overwhelming. After a lovely evening, we went to bed and slept well.

At breakfast we were visited by a number of magpies who first settled on the deck railing, then came closer on the assumption they were going to be fed. Being the intelligent birds they are, it was clear that word had got out among their community that this was a place for freebies. Once Mike had made them happy with some morsels of cheese, rainbow lorakeets and a kookaburra showed up, so they had to be catered for as well.

After breakfast there was a photo-comparing session when Janet and Pat called up pictures from the past to laugh and wonder over. It's quite surprising how many images from that period in England more than 50 years ago have been saved, even though the colour balance of the original slides had deteriorated considerably.

We drove down to the Pamboola Wet Lands and went for a very pleasant walk through farm fields and along the banks of the Pambula River. There were many waterfowl to be seen including shorebirds and ducks. The Pambula River Garden Centre was very close by so we sat down there for cups of cappuccino in a very pleasant ambiance, then checked out the adjoining art gallery. There were some nice paintings and prints, and some lovely wood carvings, but nothing that really appealed. Back at the house we had lunch and planned for the afternoon's excursion.

Killer Whale Museum

Pat and Mike had told us about the museum in Eden that was well worth a visit, so we drove some 20 kilometers west. We hadn't heard of a whaling industry in this part of the world, so the museum displays presented us with some novelties. Killer whales, or orcas, were employed by the whalers to assist in corralling their larger cousins, the fin whales and right whales. The skeleton of Old Tom, their longest serving orca, was on display and you could clearly see the deep grooves in his teeth, worn by the rope line that he gripped when serving his masters. Much to our surprise we learned that these whales would work as a team to hunt other larger whales in order to kill them for food. They would 'corral' the whale and force it into an area where they could attack it and eventually eat it. Working with humans, when the whale was caught the orcas would be given the mouth, cheek and tongue to eat, which were their favourite parts. As the orcas already had inbred hunting skills, it seemed logical to the whalers to use their skills to help with the whale hunt.

The museum displays occupied two floors and featured a large collection of whaling-related artifacts including boats, tools and apparatus. Wall-mounted display panels provided a wealth of information about the whalers of the 19th and early 20th centuries. It was very interesting to learn about the whaling here and think about what we had seen in Red Bay, Labrador several years ago. Although we have no specific information it is likely the techniques for whaling were very similar. Here though, they had the advantage of using killer whales to help them, while off the coast of Newfoundland, that was not an option. I did prefer the Red Bay exhibit because the little island the whalers used for rendering blubber could be visited, making the exhibits more immediate and allowing the visitor to actually imagine what it must have been like so many years ago.

Whaling boats are surrounded by galleries of artifacts and exhibits, all attractively laid out and described

Later that evening we went to the restaurant in the Retired Servicemen's League in Merimboola for supper. It was really lovely there, and we had a very good meal and conversation. Before we returned home, I was able to log on to WiFi at the RSL reception desk, and get the latest Corona news. Our sons David and Ian had been keeping us up to date on the virus, and had organized food for our return, so we should be good for our 14-day self isolation. All we would have to do is get home. During the day we had tried to contact Aeroplan and Air Canada with no success; they were overwhelmed with people calling them, so we would just have to keep trying.

We started off doing groceries and banking. The ATM dutifully disgorged money for me, the first time we had needed to actually get cash since we left London! We had done a trial run in Lake's Entrance, so were pleased to see it still worked. I managed to find some allergy pills. I didn't want people to think my runny nose is Corona when it was just allergy! Pat and Mike got the groceries we needed and we went back to the house to put them away before going to the beach. It was interesting to note there was no panic buying here; nobody seemed too concerned about the pandemic in this area, and maybe they were counting on being far away from the big cities and didn't expect it to touch them.

Pat and Mike had lost all their snorkelling gear in the house fire, so they were anxious to try out their new equipment. We drove to the small estuary where the Pambula River enters the sea. It was a beautiful spot, hot, clear water, sand, everything you would want from such a place. We walked up the river to a spot where the two of them felt they could both swim and test out equipment. While they headed for the water Bob and I relaxed in the sun and enjoyed watching the two of them in the water. Apparently, the river water was cold, so we were glad not to have gone in. Naturally, lots of pictures were taken, especially because it is a beautiful spot and the weather was perfect.

After lunch we a went for a walk to the Pinnacles. These are huge sandstone cliffs and are quite spectacular. The walk was a bit different from our Algonquin Park experience because there it is all rocks and roots, while this one was sand and roots. A lot easier on the feet. There were a number of steps to negotiate but not too bad. Pat and Mike are both very involved in nature conservation and have a great deal of information on the area. They told us about the introduced Eastern Pine, which is taking over from the native plants. They were happy to see many of them had been chopped down and there were large areas set aside for native plants to regrow. After this visit we drove to the oyster beds and spotted a number of pelicans on the other side of the lake, as well as the posts for the oyster fishing equipment. It was a lovely quiet spot, and I enjoyed being there.

Finally, we went home and started preparing supper. Now we were in for a treat. The birds came to play, rainbow lorakeets, magpies and a kookaburra. It was such fun watching them feed on apples and bread, and in the case of the kookaburra, pieces of chicken. Many pictures were taken, and much time spent enjoying interacting with the birds. After they left the kangaroos appeared, eating the grass and just showing off. It was a delightful display and we all enjoyed it. After supper we watched some of the pictures from Malacoota after the fire. Not pretty at all. Pat and Mike are coping with it all, and planning their new house, which they hope to have built in about a year unless Corona interferes with that plan.

We talked for ages and encouraged them to come and see us in Canada next year, if possible. It would be lovely to show them around. Tomorrow, we would leave Pambula and see how we could manage the next few days, deciding what plans we could resurrect from the pandemic.

CANBERRA

We said goodbye to Pat and Mike and the lovely house in Pambula and headed for Canberra. We drove north to Bega and then turned west. We could see the mountains in the distance in front of us and, as they spread north and south across our view, we knew it was just a matter of kilometers before we would have to climb them. The road up was quite spectacular with over 10 km of hairpins, reminding us of the drives in the Alps and Pyrenees, except this one was through thick forest. The summit came at just over 1,000 metres and instead of descending, the road remained on a high plateau. We passed through several small towns, on the lookout for a gas station, but they were small and didn't have many facilities. We made it to Cooma with plenty of fuel, stopped for more, and turned north for Canberra. The scenery of the high plateau was quite a contrast to the lowlands we had come from; smooth, rolling hills with a great deal of scrubby vegetation, ideal grazing lands for sheep and cows, of which there were many.

No matter where we drive in the entire world, we come across roadworks. Here in Australia, it seemed that the roads were in a constant state of being fixed, so plastic orange cones were everywhere. There were the same workers with the same lollipop signs as we see in North America, except they wore wide-brimmed bush hats. But the roads are much better than ours—no freeze/thaw cycle—so to our eyes they hardly needed fixing. And why is it, throughout the entire world, that the stick figure on the sign has 'floating head disease' while his lollipop is securely mounted on its stick?

We had intended to have lunch in one of the many rest-stops we had seen in Victoria, but as soon as we crossed the border into the Australian Capital Territory rest stops ceased to exist. We decided to push on to Canberra, find a motel, and eat there. As we approached the capital, we came across lots of information signs—you can't miss them: they are a bright yellow 'I' on a blue background—but none of them ever led us to an information centre. The directions would evaporate, then another would show up with the same lack of resolution. You can't miss the signs, but you can sure miss the information centres. In the end, we pulled off the highway at a place called Fyshwick and went exploring for a gas station where we could ask directions.

Enter Ben and his wife, and Endeavour Carpets. After a fruitless search for a gas station, we went three-quarters of the way round a roundabout and peeled off into an industrial area. Why not ask someone? They can only say no. As it happened, we found two wonderful people—Ben and his wife—behind the counter of their family-run carpet business. They not only helped us locate where we were, but even recommended a hotel where their reps always stayed. And if this wasn't enough, Ben's wife even phoned the hotel and made a booking for us. We thanked them for their kindness, happily found our way and checked in with no problem.

The afternoon was spent in catching up with writing, photo processing and emails, while Bob discovered that his computer had taken another snit and refused to send emails. Then it was out for the evening for dinner with our friend Dean from Ottawa and his partner Jonathan. We celebrated our reunion with two bottles from our wine-tasting expedition. It was from them we discovered that Fyshwick used to be the area of disrepute! Had we known that we might have explored more than just the carpet store!

The four of us went out for supper at a little Italian restaurant, where Jonathan noted that the tables were too close together, and not following the new normal of social distancing. It was a lovely meal and we had a wonderful time with the guys. Over dinner Jonathan wrote out a long list of things to see in Canberra. Hopefully, next time they are in Ottawa we will get together and not have to worry about 'social distancing.'

Now we needed to cover some of Jonathan's long list. The first stop in our drive was the National Capital Exhibition where we parked the car and watched the enormous fountain in Lake Burley Griffin. We learned later that we had been quite lucky to see it as it was only run for a couple of hours a day and had only begun just recently because of a prolonged drought. Then

we made out way to the Visitor Center. For the first time on this visit, we actually followed and found that elusive entity, The Information Centre, which was located in Commonwealth Park.

By this time, we were overdue for lunch so we asked the two ladies at the information desk where we could eat, and they gave directions for a cafe in the National Portrait Gallery across the lake. After chatting with them for some time we bought two gifts for our granddaughters before heading back to the car. We drove across the Commonwealth Avenue bridge to the administrative side of Canberra and made out way to the National Portrait Gallery for our lunch.

The National Portrait Gallery is in a fine modern building fronted by a waterway that cascades in steps. While we wanted to see the portraits, lunch and a cup of tea were becoming urgent necessities. They served very good lunch food and the leaf tea came in little pots with strainers in the top. As it was quite late in the afternoon by this time, the refreshment was very welcome. Now for the portraits. The early explorers such as James Cook and Joseph Banks were well represented, and there was a series of wide-ranging portraits of the men and women who opened Australia. Portraits of Aboriginals were also present, and in another gallery Aboriginal art was displayed. This was a very extensive collection and excellently displayed.

As time was becoming tight, we decided we'd drive up to the top of Mount Ainslie where there would be a view over the whole of Canberra. Looking at the map, this seemed fairly straightforward, but when we tried it, we ended up driving round in circles. The inner and outer circles of the roads around Capital Hill don't necessarily lead into each other. After a few wrong

turns, we stopped to consult the map in front of the Old Parliament Building, now the Museum of Australian Democracy. This is a fine white building with a profusion of flags on masts; a nice place to stop and gain bearings.

Once we clarified the map, we found the Anzac Memorial and then it was plain sailing. Our poor little car was tired and felt the strain of going up yet another hill, but we made it. We passed a number of cyclists on the way up, some were successful while others were pushing their bikes. my sympathies were with them. The view from the top was fantastic; at 843 metres it dominates the city. The top of the hill was laid out with walkways, belvederes and platforms so you could get views from several vantage points. Seeing Canberra this way we could finally understand the geo-

metrical layout, and with the large information panel realized the thoughts about planning this city. It would appear the town planners were thinking about people and not density. How it stands up now, many years after I'm not so sure. Certainly, the government areas of town are beautifully planned and cared for, but we don't know how the impact of increasing population has changed the suburbs.

We returned to our hotel, caught up with a bit of writing, then finished the evening at a nice little Indian restaurant a short walk away. The following day we would be back to Sydney, and then the continuing efforts to see if we can reschedule our flights before Air Canada closed down completely. It continued to be impossible to contact Air Canada or Aeroplan, but David was working on it as well.

Great news came at 6:00 a.m. David emailed us to say that he had got through to Aeroplan after being on hold for three hours, and had re-booked us for Wednesday the 25th on All Nippon Airways to Tokyo then Chicago, and onward to Montreal by Air Canada. The relief was amazing. Sleep the night before had not been good.

Chapter Twelve: Sydney and Return Home

We left Canberra after breakfast and headed north to Sydney. We were intending to stop one night somewhere en route but decided we would be better off being in Sydney. There we would have reliable internet and could update the blog, which was now many days in arrears. We had had no WiFi in the house in Pambula, while in Canberra Bob's little computer would only accept emails, but refused to send them. On the way to Sydney, we stopped at our final winery, Cherry Tree Hill, over the border in New South Wales. We tried a few of their wines, were not very impressed, but ended up with a Merlot that we would enjoy glass by glass each evening in Sydney. We were also able to find some lovely fruit at a stall in a gas station. We bought enough to keep us happy until we left.

We dropped off the car at the airport but found nobody at the desk to receive it. After wandering the parking garage for a while, we loaded the luggage onto a cart and went to check at the Enterprise desk. There was nobody there either, so after some more waiting around Bob went back to the parking and found an operative who said to just drop the key in the slot. Meanwhile, a lady came by and advised the same thing, only we were not sure if she was an Enterprise employee as she took off right away. She did go behind the desk for the 'We are away from the desk and will be back in 15 mins' sign and put it on the counter, and then left. It would have been helpful to have had that sign displayed when we arrived! A subsequent phone call revealed that they had charged us twice for the rental, and that because we'd brought it back late there was no one-day rebate. Well, at least it was worth phoning. The service here was not what would get in Ottawa, so we really were surprised, but perhaps the pandemic threat was trickling down?

The taxi stands were empty of passengers, so getting a taxi was easy. Our taxi driver to the hotel was a Ghanaian from Kumasi, and one with a great sense of humour. He complained about the lack of fares and told us he had been sitting at the taxi rank for hours waiting for anyone to pick up, but it was all done with laughs and joking. He was amused at the hoarding of toilet paper and said, 'If you didn't have food what was the point of looking after the other end?' Bob told him we have lots of books. If you can't laugh, he said, what can you do? We gave him a little extra for the amusement he'd given us on the ride.

We checked into the Intercontinental Hotel, went up to our room, and spread our stuff around. Bob's little computer decided it still didn't like connecting to the hotel WiFi, so it went into a monumental sulk. He was contemplating taking it down to Circular Quay and skipping it over the waves in one mighty swing of the arm.

Once we were settled, we went for a walk through the Botanical Gardens. When we were in the gardens, we noticed many people walking around, and small groups coming together. This surprised us, as we thought with all the talk of social distancing, we wouldn't see that. In one area there was obviously a fairly large wedding party, celebrating the happy occasion. While we recognized the wish to celebrate such an important event, we just hope nobody involved was infected with Corona.

We ended up in Circular Quay and walked around. It was a complete dead zone, very few people, hardly anyone in the cafes, just like Singapore. Bob spoke to a street artist for a little while, and he said this was likely his last day here, because he wasn't making enough. Very sad. When you realize how many people this shut down affects it is really scary. We did stop in our favourite creperie, which was very empty, only a couple of patrons. We did say we would come back the next day if it were open. The manager was not even sure about that.

Finally, we made it back to the hotel and had supper in a very underpopulated bar/café; six patrons while we were there! Every second table had a reserve sign on it in order to ensure social distancing. It all felt very sad. Once back in our room it was time to start catching up with our writing and then enjoy a glass of wine as we played a nice game of Schotten Totten, a crazy card game.

Bob overdid breakfast in the hotel dining room. How was he to know that French toast with Nutella and bananas would be covered in a thick, toffee-like sauce that pulled away in sticky hanging threads? It should have been impossible to eat, but that didn't stop him cleaning the plate. The sad thing about the hotel in general was the emptiness of it all, and this was evident in the dining room where it wasn't necessary to provide 'social distancing' according to the advice. We were 'socially distanced' by being almost the only people in the dining room. The hotel staff we spoke to were all worried about their jobs, and many had been laid off already.

JUSTICE AND POLICE MUSEUM

We had seen the Sydney's 'home of crime' nearby, housed in the old courthouse and police station. We had found that it was only open on weekends, so this was our opportunity. We decided to take what precautions we could and wore our face masks for going out of doors. It was interesting that very few other people on the street were masked, and those we did see wore the lightweight ones. It appeared that people in Sydney were not yet taking things really seriously.

There was a large notice in the entrance of the museum about COVID-19 and we were asked when we had arrived in Sydney and if we had come off a cruise ship. This is becoming the norm for public buildings. Once we assured the staff we had been in Australia for a few weeks, they gave us tickets and a map of the displays. The first gallery was called City of Shadows and featured slide shows of selected images from a huge cache of police photographs from the 1920s and '30s. In the cells, each of which was fitted out with displays, we could see weapons, police equipment, safe-breaking tools, and features of notorious criminals such as Ned Kelly. There were mugshots of criminals, accompanied by descriptions of their crimes, and pictures of crime scenes and accidents. All very disturbing.

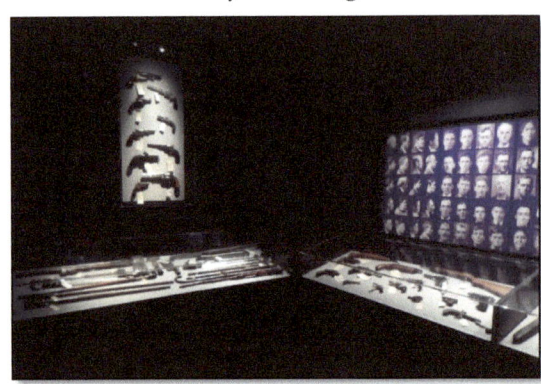

Confiscated weapons and mugshots on display in one of the cells. In the last days in our hotel, pacing the floors, we empathized with those incarcerated souls

In the centre of the cell block were two criminal courts, one of which was for the Water Police, a separate division. In the first court there was a high raised bench for the judge, rows of lower benches for the jury, public, witnesses, etc., and a large wrought iron cage for the accused. The Water Court was similar but had no cage. Perhaps the crimes tried here were not so severe? The tour of the building finished with displays of notorious criminals, and there were lots of them in this ex-penal colony.

After our museum visit, we went shopping for a few grocery supplies, and we found the shop where we had bought the little wheelie for our Alice Springs excursion. There we found a nice little shoulder bag that would be ideal for carrying our supply of face masks, wipes and other necessities. We are taking this seriously. We returned to the hotel, had an impromptu lunch, and spent the afternoon writing. For supper we decided to visit the Four Frogs crêperie, which was still open but virtually empty, but likely closing the next day. We found this all very saddening and could only guess at the ripple effect this was having through the entire economy. What were these people going to do?

In the evening, we finally got another blog launched, so the followers would know we were still around, and then we had a game of Jaipur over another glass of that wine from Cherry Hill. Breakfast was a lonely affair with only a few hotel guests in the large dining room. The buffet end of the room looked very forlorn with its empty service hatch and tables. All dining was a-la-carte and to judge from the time it took, each meal was clearly prepared from scratch, which was not such a bad thing. We were not sure how many guests were left in the hotel, but we figured there were very few.

One of the saddest things we had to do was cancel our trip to the Great Barrier Reef, and forgo a night in an underwater hotel. The hotel owners were very understanding and refunded our deposit, which we really appreciated. When we called Qantas about our cancelled flights, there was no refund because we had booked though an agent! We were annoyed but at that point could do nothing. Several years later we did receive a notice from Qantas that our airfares would finally be refunded! It was late, but it did finally come.

By now all the restaurants in the hotel were closed, so all our meals were from room service. Our only activities were maintaining the blog and taking some exercise walking the halls on our floor. Sadly, this was a safe activity because we were the only ones on the floor! So, every couple of hours we would take turns walking around the 'block!' There was no thought of going outside the building until it was time to go.

Since our flight was the next day, it was time to start thinking about packing all our bags and belongings so we would be ready to leave. It was a long and tedious day, but we were lucky we had our tickets, we were going home, and didn't have think of Australia being our new home, however 'interesting' that might have been.

RETURN HOME

We spent the morning in the hotel, and then at 1.00 p.m. we made our way to the airport by taxi, early but better than sitting around drumming our fingers. The traffic was light, and the trip much faster than usual, likely due to so many people working from home. Just a sign of the times. When we arrived at the airport, we met a couple outside the terminal with all their baggage. Their flight had been cancelled. They were due to fly back to the UK via Singapore, but Singapore had been closed to in-transit flights for several days, and British Airways or their travel agent had not notified them.

Now they were at the airport with no flight, no information about any other booking, and no accommodation! They would have to return to the hotel where they had been staying and hopefully sort it out. We went into the airport, thankfully knowing we had a booked flight. It felt so different this time. It was packed with worried people try to find a flight out of Sydney to their home base. The anxiety was tangible, so different from the usual excitement of people looking forward to travelling to exotic places.

We were slightly more relaxed, thanks to David's hard work. We were booked through Tokyo to Chicago and then on to Montreal. Our first flight was at 6:00 p.m., so we had plenty of time to kill. Thank goodness for our masks, given to us so long ago in Thailand, as well as the hand sanitizer that came along with them. While we were sitting down various people came and went. Two young women from Sweden were desperately trying to get home, phoning, checking for flights on-line, and going to the flight centre just to try to find a way home. They hadn't found a flight while we were there, but we just hoped they eventually did.

Finally, it was time for us to check in and go through security. Once in the departure lounge, we could more or less relax as we knew we would be on our way soon. We were going to be a couple of days in transit, but at least we were going home, although from all we had read we were worried about the screening at the other end. What would happen it they thought we were sick? While we felt well, we didn't want to think about becoming sick during our flights. The flights themselves were lovely. We were on All Nippon Airways, a half-empty overnight flight, which was most luxurious. The flight attendants were very attentive. After a beautifully served meal, it was time to settle down. Bob and I both slept for some time—we really needed that. The odd thing about this flight was no breakfast. Orange juice only, but in retrospect I am sure if we had asked for something to eat, they would have provided it. When we arrived in Tokyo, we found our way to the ANA lounge, and relaxed as much as we could, as well as getting something to eat and drink. Even there, there was a limited amount of food and drink on offer, and no hot food service at all. At that point it really didn't matter; we were luckier than many others as we were on our way home!

Due to a previous illness, my tolerance for walking through airports was limited, so we had requested a wheelchair, so I would be able to get to the boarding gate on time. Everyone was very kind and helped me on my way. On the plane itself I was cared for and all my needs met, not that I needed much! This next flight to O'Hare airport in Chicago was a long one: 12 hours coupled to an exceptionally long day. For me, it felt like much more than 24 hours, due to all the time changes along the way. We were going back in time, not forward. Very weird.

Once in Chicago we were met with a wheelchair. We were amused; the chair in Tokyo had been quite small, while the one in Chicago was much larger, and I could have shared it with another person! The wonderful thing was being taken through all the bureaucracy quickly and easily, fast tracked with our documents. We were told that we were one of only five flights that had come into O'Hare that day! It emphasized the effect COVID was having on everything.

Then onto the shuttle bus to the next terminal, where Air Canada was situated. Bob spoke to the staff there and they kindly rerouted us through Toronto to Montreal on earlier flights. They rescued our baggage, and generally sorted us out. So now off to Montreal. Due to COVID-19, Air Canada was not serving food, just a bottle of water, which was fine. Just over an hour later we landed in Toronto. Now came the worrying bit: The screening. We didn't need to worry. There were several Border Control officers at the top of the escalators, and they asked us where we were from, did we know about self-isolation, and here's a leaflet about it! No temperature check, no questions on our health, nothing! In Kolkata, more than a month ago, they had checked our temperature continually, and the same in Chiang Mai, but not in Toronto.

Immigration and Customs were quickly done, no issues. Our bags were going onto Montreal, so it was just a customs declaration, and then on our way. Again, no health checks at all. The flight to Montreal was quick, and our bags were already at the carrousel when we arrived. All we had to do now was get to our hotel for the night and drive home the next day. The hotel was within the terminal itself, so it very smooth and easy. It was eerie to be walking through a completely empty arrivals area; not a soul in sight. The difficult part came a bit later as the hotel kitchen wasn't working, so Bob had to go back down to the terminal to find food, which he did from one single stall that was still open. A bath, a glass of wine and bed. A good end to a very long two days.

The next morning, we found the car that Ian had brought to Montreal and parked for us. We swabbed all sorts of surfaces with the sanitary wipes he had provided, and thankfully drove home. We got to our lovely house which was stocked with supplies bought by Ian and Mandy, to last us through the quarantine period.

We were finally home and could relax after the very different airline experience and start to think about all we had seen and done over the last three months. It had been an amazing adventure, we had seen and learned a lot, and although the final few days were difficult, even those were a learning experience. The sad part of coming home during the pandemic was being unable to spend time with family and friends and tell them about our adventures. However, we have a small balcony on our bedroom, so at least we could tie the gifts we had brought them on a string, and lower them down to those waiting on the driveway.